'It has always struck me that Historical Portrait Galleries far transcend in worth all other kinds of National Collections of Pictures whatever; that in fact they ought to exist … in every country, as among the most popular and cherished National Possessions … if Scotland be the first to set an example in that respect, Scotland will do honourably by herself, and achieve a benefit to all the world'.

Thomas Carlyle writing to David Laing in 1854

Duncan Thomson

A HISTORY OF THE SCOTTISH NATIONAL PORTRAIT GALLERY

National Galleries of Scotland
Edinburgh 2011

Published by the Trustees of the National Galleries of
Scotland in celebration of the re-opening of the Scottish
National Portrait Gallery in December 2011

Text: © the Trustees of the National Galleries of Scotland

ISBN 978 1 906270 48 3

Front cover: Scottish National Portrait Gallery
photographed by Keith Hunter

Back cover: Scottish National Portrait Gallery
photographed by Henry Bedford Lemere

Inside flap: John Ritchie Findlay by W. Graham Boss

Frontispiece: Scottish National Portrait Gallery
by Thomas Crawford Hamilton, 1890

Designed and typeset in Minion by Dalrymple
Printed on Chromomat 150gsm by Die Keure, Belgium
Bound in Toile du Marais kindly sponsored
by Winter & Company

The proceeds from this book go towards supporting the
National Galleries of Scotland. For a complete list of current
publications, please write to NGS Publishing, 75 Belford Road,
Edinburgh EH4 3DR, or visit our website:
www.nationalgalleries.org

National Galleries of Scotland is a charity
registered in Scotland (no.SC003728)

NATIONAL
GALLERIES
SCOTLAND

CONTENTS

FOREWORD

This book celebrates the history of the Scottish National Portrait Gallery and marks its re-opening in December 2011 after major refurbishment. Written by Dr Duncan Thomson, Keeper of the Portrait Gallery from 1982 to 1997, it charts the progress of one of Scotland's great national institutions. Housed in a remarkable Victorian building and adorned with sculpture that proclaims its purpose to the world, the Portrait Gallery has an unrivalled collection of Scotland's national portraits. Indeed, there are very few Scots of note not represented in some way in its collection. For assistance with this book, Dr Duncan Thomson would like to thank Janis Adams, Robert Dalrymple, John Dick, Imogen Gibbon, Robin Hutchison, Helen Smailes, Giles Waterfield, and, especially, Julia Thomson.

The recent renovation has been generously funded by the Scottish Government, the Heritage Lottery Fund, the Monument Trust and very many other donors from Scotland and across the world. It has allowed the Portrait Gallery to occupy the whole of the building originally designed for it by Sir Robert Rowand Anderson in the 1880s. With displays ranging from the Reformation through to our own times, the entire concept of a Portrait Gallery for Scotland has been reinvented for a contemporary audience. The refurbishment has also permitted the introduction of those modern services that today's visitors rightly expect. From its base in Queen Street, in the heart of Edinburgh, the Portrait Gallery works across the nation, and internationally, through its programmes, exhibitions and loans.

This book has been made possible by a bequest from the late Miss Mary Legget Bowman, a frequent visitor who loved the Scottish National Portrait Gallery. It is hoped that Miss Bowman's generosity will encourage many others to learn more about this remarkable building and the unique collection contained in it.

JOHN LEIGHTON
Director-General, National Galleries of Scotland

JAMES HOLLOWAY
Director, Scottish National Portrait Gallery

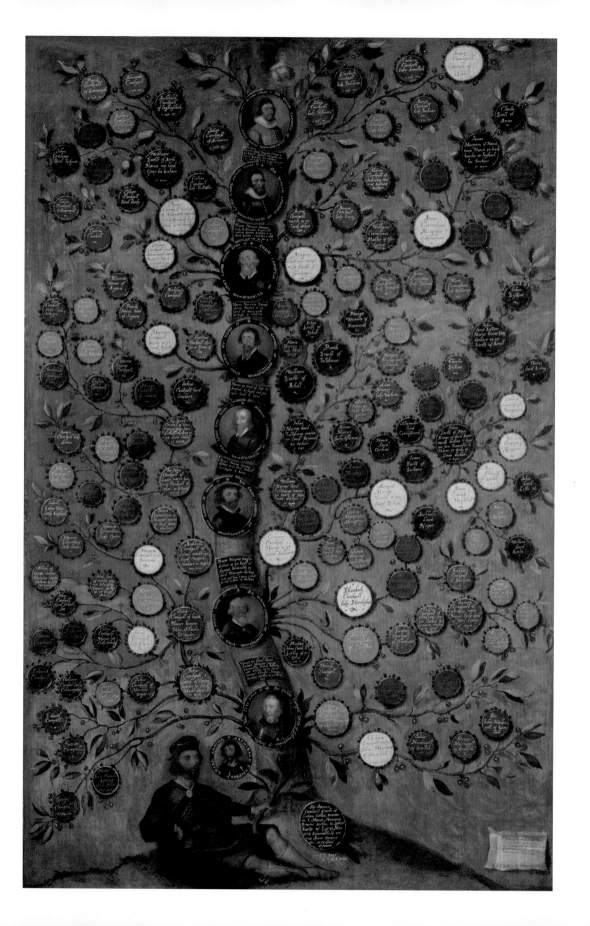

CHAPTER ONE

A PORTRAIT GALLERY
FOR THE NATION

IN the summer of 1633 the city of Edinburgh welcomed King Charles I with a public display of portraits of his royal ancestors. The king made his triumphal entry for his long-delayed Scottish coronation from the west, and, having been given the keys to the city gate beneath the towering castle rock, he proceeded to the High Street. Here, either on the façades of the tall, closely encompassing tenements, or on a triumphal arch through which Charles passed, a gallery of portraits of his 109 predecessors had been set up. Some, or perhaps all, were the work of the country's first significant portrait painter, George Jamesone. The portraits were almost certainly freshly minted – and mainly freshly imagined, for there were pre-existing images of only the king's most immediate forebears. The mythical parts of the lineage, stretching back into a deep and unknown past, were well established and accepted as the truth. It was a portrait gallery that proclaimed the longevity and the legitimacy of the royal line – something that was divinely ordained.

In the sixteenth and seventeenth centuries Scotland's links with the Low Countries were close, and the use of portraits in this way as part of a 'joyous entry' must have been derived from these northern neighbours. Portraits as emblems of individual identity in the modern sense, however, had grown from the sometimes intrusive presence of identifiable donors in the painted altarpieces of Renaissance Italy in the previous century, where he who paid had himself linked with the eternal. In turn, individual portraits would become the material of historical series, those groups known as *uomini famosi* – famous men – that spoke of human achievement and the effects of time.

This need to preserve a semblance of the past by means of images of human likeness, something deeply rooted in the psyche, is attested by a type of portrait of a far earlier origin than these, and curiously overlooked in the history of portraiture because it did not fit a standard model of belief in progress in the arts: the Romano-Egyptian portraits that were painted in the Fayum district of Egypt in the first century. These life-size heads, many of them certainly painted from life, may originally have hung on walls, but were preserved – as the identity of their subjects, some known, others now unnamed, has been ever since – by being attached to the mummified remains of their bodies. Their realism is startling evidence of the power of portraiture to make the past tangible and credible, to say 'this is how it was'.

The display that was set up in Edinburgh to remind Charles where he had come from set a new fashion in Scotland, or at least stirred a feeling that was already nascent, for in the years immediately following his visit the Highlander Sir Colin Campbell of Glenorchy created a gallery of his own ancestors in his castle at Finlarig. These portraits were the work of George Jamesone and a much cruder,

[9]

unidentified immigrant painter. But Campbell's gallery had wider pretensions and he added portraits of contemporaries with whom his family was linked, painted from life by Jamesone. In addition, the artist supplied him with another series of Scottish monarchs and embodied Campbell's own lineage in an extraordinary painting of his family tree [1]. This spirit of both personal and national assertion was still alive as late as the 1680s, when portraits of 111 monarchs by the Dutch painter Jacob de Wet (many derived from Jamesone's set) were placed in the long gallery of the royal palace of Holyroodhouse by its hereditary keeper, the Duke of Hamilton.

The largest gallery of 'famous men' in Scotland was amassed in the latter part of the seventeenth century by Robert Kerr, 1st Marquess of Lothian, at Newbattle Abbey, just south of Edinburgh. His gallery was far more widely ranging, and spanned both British and European history with varying degrees of authenticity. Many of the portraits were supplied by the Parisian painter Louis-Ferdinand Elle (including a large version of Frans Hals's little portrait of the philosopher René Descartes). In the early years of the eighteenth century the Newbattle gallery was being claimed as 'a better room than the King's new gallery for pictures at Kensington'. By this time the collection also included twenty-five of the Scottish monarchs that Jamesone had painted for Charles I's entry to Edinburgh. The whole collection remained intact in one form or another until the middle of the twentieth century, and it provides a direct link with the sentiment that would lead to the founding of the Scottish National Portrait Gallery. Among those later members of the Kerr family who lived with this vivid exposition of the past was Schomberg Henry Kerr, the 9th Marquess of Lothian, who was to be one of those most deeply involved in the creation of the Portrait Gallery. Diplomat and politician, it was as an active and long serving President of the Society of Antiquaries of Scotland that he played this role. It is difficult to believe that his enthusiasm for that project was not coloured by living in such surroundings.

The need to comprehend the past, and make it a stepping-stone to the future, is the motive force that has driven the conception of national portrait galleries, firstly in Europe in the nineteenth century and recently across the world. That London was the powerhouse of the greatest empire ever seen, and the focus of ideas of almost limitless progress, was no doubt a crucial factor, when allied to these pro-founder motives, in the formation of its National Portrait Gallery in 1856. It was followed in 1882 by another city within that empire, when the Scottish National Portrait Gallery was founded in Edinburgh. For a time they were lone examples, but portrait galleries of a national kind embedded in other types of national collections came into being in Dublin in Ireland, at the castle of Gripsholm in Sweden and at Frederiksborg Castle in Denmark. Much later, in 1960, a national portrait gallery on what had by then come to be seen as traditional lines was opened in Washington in the United States, sharing a building with American art, but distinct. Then followed national portrait galleries in New Zealand (1988) and Australia (1993). More recently the concept has been under consideration in France and Canada.

Although Scotland just failed to be the first in this story, there is evidence that

both the emotional and the intellectual foundations of a national portrait gallery were being laid there earlier than elsewhere, in the latter decades of the eighteenth century. Even then, the end was clearly envisaged and only the means were lacking. It was, however, within the context of the Society of Antiquaries of Scotland, founded in 1780, and its dedication to gathering up what could be gleaned of Scotland's past, that a clear vision of a gallery of national portraits emerged.

THE ROLE OF THE SOCIETY OF ANTIQUARIES OF SCOTLAND

The Society of Antiquaries of Scotland came into being following a meeting of 'Noblemen and Gentlemen' at the house of David Stewart Erskine, 11th Earl of Buchan, in St Andrew Square in Edinburgh in 1780 [2]. By 1782 a royal charter was being sought and, with the help of Henry Dundas, Secretary of State for 'the Northern Department' (a definition of Scotland that sat uncomfortably with the kind of Scottish identity that the Society represented), this was achieved the following year. At the initial meeting, Lord Buchan was unambiguously designated 'founder'. Curiously, a number of former Jacobites, including the Abbé Grant and Andrew Lumisden who had been secretary to the Young Pretender, Charles Edward Stuart, were enrolled as honorary members. Others included the *philosophe* Diderot and the future statesman William Pitt.

The Earl of Buchan was an enthusiast in the same mould as his near contemporary, Sir John Sinclair of Ulbster, each obsessive and sometimes insufferable,

2 *David Stewart Erskine, 11th Earl of Buchan* by John Brown, 1781
Gifted by the Society of Antiquaries of Scotland in 2009, PG 3596

3 *Sir William Wallace* by the 11th Earl of Buchan
W.F. Watson Bequest in 1886, PG 1616

but both resolutely dedicated to retrieving Scotland's past. Sinclair had joined the Society in 1787 and when Buchan was forced to resign from the Society in 1790 (apparently because he had promised financial help that he was unable to deliver), Sinclair succeeded him as Vice-President and served until 1797. In these years Sinclair was publishing the many volumes of his great *Statistical Account of Scotland*, an attempt to draw together the historical, social and economic life of Scotland. This was in its way an early 'portrait of a nation'. Written mainly by the country's parish ministers and edited by Sinclair, it was a characterisation of a country that, in its comprehensiveness and scale, was unparalleled for its time anywhere in Europe.

It is through the eyes of a major player in the later history of the Society, David Laing, who was also an important promoter of the idea of a national collection of portraits, that an intimate picture of Lord Buchan can be gained. While referring to Buchan's 'extraordinary personal vanity' and his 'complete and unconscious ... self-deception', Laing nevertheless found him 'a kind-hearted, loveable person'. Laing describes Buchan's urge towards a collection, or collections, of national portraiture:

> One of his favourite schemes in connexion with this Society was to establish a gallery of original portraits of illustrious and learned Scotsmen, under the high-sounding title of the Caledonian Temple of Fame; but the process of selecting those thought worthy of admission [a complex balloting system of subjects who must have been dead for at least 25 years] was simply ridiculous. At the bank of the River Tweed ... he erected a huge colossal figure ... of the patriot Chieftain, Sir William Wallace. He devoted a large hall within the ruins of Dryburgh Abbey ... to serve as a 'Temple of Glory' consisting of fragmentary stones ... and a series of brackets, bearing a number of plaster busts and casts of eminent men ...

Like many at the time, Buchan was also a compiler of lists, and by 1781 he had prepared a manuscript for the Society of Antiquaries enumerating the portraits of 'Illustrious and Learned Scots' which he knew about. He was aided in his researches by the fact that he was an accomplished draughtsman, having received training at the Foulis Academy, a school of art and design, set up within the University of Glasgow by the printers and publishers Robert and Andrew Foulis. Buchan used this skill to make copy-drawings of historical portraits in the private collections of Scotland to which, by his social position, he had easy access. A large number of these drawings are still in the Portrait Gallery's collection [3]. These images were turned into a kind of 'gallery' and disseminated by means of two publications where they were reproduced in engraved form: the *Iconographia Scotica* of 1797, and the *Scottish Gallery; or Portraits of Eminent Persons of Scotland ... with brief accounts of the Characters represented* which was published in 1799. Laing, rightly, had no great opinion of the rather coarse engravings, but they were a valuable record, and some remain so. The 'brief accounts' were the work of the historian and antiquarian John Pinkerton, with whom Buchan pursued a detailed correspondence on questions of authenticity. This combination of biography and iconography loomed large in all the endeavours of this kind, presaging the approach of historians like Thomas Carlyle, and was not all that different from the course that future national portrait galleries would pursue.

The years following Lord Buchan's departure from the Society of Antiquaries were punctuated by financial problems, apathy, and a protracted search for suitable premises. At various times the Society and its collections were lodged in houses in the Cowgate, the Canongate, the Lawnmarket, the Castlehill, and George Street. Despite keeping their museum in these various premises open to the public (on application), they received no government subsidy – something they did not fail to contrast with their English and European counterparts. In 1826, however, the Society found premises as a tenant of the Board of Manufactures in that body's recently erected Royal Institution building on the Mound, adjacent to Princes Street.

The Board of Manufactures, more correctly the Board of Trustees for Fisheries and Manufactures, was an odd remnant of government administration set up in 1727 after the union of the English and Scottish parliaments twenty years earlier. Its original function had been the promotion of certain industries in Scotland – 'herring, linen and hemp [and] coarse wool' – and the improvement of industrial design, particularly in linen goods. For this purpose it had founded an art school as early as 1760, the so-called Trustees Academy, predecessor of Scotland's art colleges. As its original purpose became more tenuous it acquired a general responsibility for art affairs in Scotland, and in 1826 it erected the classical building in the Doric style that became known as the Royal Institution. This name derived from the Royal Institution for the Encouragement of the Fine Arts whose exhibitions of old master paintings were housed in the building along with the art school. (Much later, and confusingly, it became known as the Royal Scottish Academy when that body was transferred there in 1911 from rooms in the Scottish National Gallery which it had occupied since 1859.)

However, due to the continuing poor state of their finances the Society of Antiquaries had been forced to quit the Royal Institution building in 1844, and it was not until 1859 when they made over their collections to the government in exchange for free accommodation in the same building that a relatively stable future was assured. The government also awarded them an annual grant of £300 so they could employ 'a proper staff of officers'. It was at this time that the term 'National Museum of Antiquities' began to be used. All of these earlier problems over accommodation are a portent of a later search for better premises, first in the new Museum of Science and Art in Chambers Street (later the Royal Scottish Museum), and latterly in the Scottish National Portrait Gallery, where they finally alighted in 1891.

Throughout the difficult earlier years of the Society it was largely through the efforts of David Laing that it was kept, in his words, 'from becoming quite dormant'. From 1836 to 1852 he acted as Treasurer, although he did not consider himself particularly suited to the post. It was two years after he gave up this position that Laing entered into a correspondence with the great Victorian historian, Thomas Carlyle, which produced the latter's famous letter on the value of portraits. This document, once Laing had presented it to the Society of Antiquaries, became one of the two founding 'charters' of the Scottish National Portrait Gallery.

In his enterprise as historian Carlyle found that 'one of the most primary wants [was] to procure a bodily likeness of the personage inquired after; a good Portrait, if such exists; failing that, even an indifferent if sincere one'. He continued: 'Often I have found a Portrait superior in real instruction to half-a-dozen written "Biographies" … or rather, let me say, I have found that the Portrait was a small lighted candle by which the Biographies could for the first time be read, and some interpretation be made of them …' He went on: 'It has always struck me that Historical Portrait Galleries far transcend in worth all other kinds of National Collections of Pictures whatever; that in fact they ought to exist … in every country, as among the most popular and cherished National Possessions …' It is not clear which 'Portrait Galleries' Carlyle had in mind, for he notes that 'in no country is there at present such a thing to be found', which was certainly true in the modern sense. But he certainly envisaged some kind of popular, accessible gallery, expressing to Laing his 'hope [that] you in Scotland, in the "New National Museum" we hear talk of [The National Gallery], will have a good eye to this, and remedy it in your own case … if Scotland be the first to set an example in that respect, Scotland will do honourably by herself, and achieve a benefit to all the world'.

Carlyle, born the son of a stonemason in Ecclefechan in Dumfriesshire, was an immensely influential thinker in Victorian Britain [4]. His views on how 'the world's history' was shaped by the great rather than the common man were explored in the vibrant, tortured prose of a series of six public lectures delivered in 1840 and published the following year under the title, *On Heroes, Hero-Worship and the Heroic in History*. His views on 'Great Men' can easily be characterised now as idealist, sexist and Euro-centric, but they coloured, and were coloured by, the spirit of a society creating a worldwide empire. In the event, Scotland was not the first to realise the vision Carlyle expressed to Laing, for a 'British Historical Portrait Gallery' (the National Portrait Gallery) was founded by Parliament in 1856, to be housed in a series of unsatisfactory premises in London for the next forty years. The year following its foundation, Carlyle became a trustee.

Laing had solicited Carlyle's letter on a visit to the historian in London, and when he presented it to the Society he reported that Carlyle had said he could make whatever use he liked of it. Carlyle had also added in a covering letter that it would give him 'real pleasure if the project do take root, and one day come to perfection in sight of all the world'. What has been overlooked is that the oft-quoted parts of the letter were followed by a remarkably prescient description of how a portrait gallery – or an exhibition of portraits, for he does not clearly distinguish between them – should be set up and managed. His paradigm is not so very different from what eventually transpired in the two British portrait galleries. Great zeal and industry, he said, would be required in hunting down the most important portraits in the country's private collections, allied to 'the best Pictorial judgment' and 'all the Historical knowledge and good sense' that was available. He was emphatic

4 *Thomas Carlyle*
by John Linnell, 1844
Presented by Mrs Riches
in 1919, PG 893

5 *Edinburgh from the Castle* by David Roberts, about 1846

Scottish National Gallery, Edinburgh
Bought in 2002, D 5508

that there should be no living subjects (a view that profoundly coloured future attitudes) and it was necessary to be chary about people who had died in the past twenty-five years – a generation was needed 'to discriminate between popular monstrosities and Historical realities in the matter …'. There should be no modern pictures of historical events – he hated the lack of authenticity in paintings like David Wilkie's *John Knox Preaching*, and commented that such 'indisputable chaff ought to be severely purged away'.

Carlyle also raised the question of multiple representation, and proposed an answer not all that different from what prevailed. Of earlier historical figures 'all that could be found genuine' should be collected, while of more recent figures one would generally be enough – but it would all depend on quality and 'house-room'. He then tries to define 'Who is a Historical Character?' It is, in his reckoning, 'whoever lives in the memory of Scotchmen' (in Carlyle's view if we have a memory we are all historians). He then gives what, for him, seems to be a remarkably democratic list of the kind of person who might be included: 'a conspicuous worker, speaker, singer, or sufferer in the past time of Scotland'.

Carlyle went on to stress the importance of the catalogue 'as one of the best parts of the whole'. It is a description that certainly influenced the early publications of the Portrait Gallery (he imagined them well-produced, but cheaply, and available in railway stations) and their content is not far from what after many years became the norm in wall-labelling. The emphasis should be on brevity, the 'essence of the man's history, condensed to the very utmost … the bones of his history'. Reference should be made to sources and, perhaps more surprisingly, the provenance of the portrait should be given, for it should not be forgotten that the thing itself has a history. However, despite his taking account of artistic quality in a number of his statements, no reference is made to the artist and the intrinsic qualities of the image – again something that portrait galleries have tended to follow.

David Laing had no intention of pressing the Society of Antiquaries to take responsibility for realising Carlyle's concept, though he had himself collected a group of twenty-six portraits 'as the nucleus of a National Gallery of Scottish Historical Portraits', which he bequeathed to the Society at his death in 1878. It was always clear to Laing, however, that if anything were to be done, it would have to be under the umbrella of the Board of Manufactures who already had a building, the Royal Institution, which was fully in use – the Society of Antiquaries itself taking up the principal room. The Board was also at this time involved, at the government's behest, in the erection of another building on the Mound, the Scottish National Gallery, which the Treasury had approved in 1849 with the condition that £15,000 of the total cost of £40,000 should come from the Board's own funds. This project advanced in stages and was not completed until 1859. A little later, in 1861, work began on the directly government-funded Museum of Science and Art in Chambers Street and would proceed in phases until the late 1880s. In these

6 *Edinburgh Castle, the Scottish National Gallery and the Free Church College* by unknown German artist, late nineteenth century

Scottish National Gallery, Edinburgh
Bought in 2002, P 3065

circumstances there was neither the cash nor the will to create another gallery, dedicated to national portraits [5–7].

Nevertheless, for a nation imbued with ideas of almost endless economic, moral and spiritual progress, the stories and images of those who had brought Britain to this stage of its history could only increase in interest. In the same year that the National Portrait Gallery in London came into being, an exhibition of some 200 portraits was held in Aberdeen. More truly national were the three vast loan exhibitions of portraits held in South Kensington in the years 1865, 1866 and 1867. A similar exhibition, though more local in interest, was held in Glasgow in 1868, while in 1876 the Board of Trustees mounted a celebratory exhibition of some 325 portraits by Henry Raeburn in the Royal Institution building.

7 *The National Gallery and the Royal Institution (now the Royal Scottish Academy)* by William Donaldson Clark, about 1858

Given by Mrs Riddell in memory of Peter Fletcher Riddell in 1985, PGP R 128

THE FOUNDING OF THE SCOTTISH NATIONAL PORTRAIT GALLERY

In 1873 the Society of Antiquaries elected a new Fellow, John Ritchie Findlay. Findlay, not yet fifty, was the highly successful owner of *The Scotsman* newspaper and already a trustee of the Board of Manufactures. Although a comfortably embedded member of the Scottish establishment of the day, he had radical leanings – he had been a friend of the opium eater, Thomas de Quincey, and was an active supporter of the admission of women to medical education. Findlay quickly became an office-bearer in the Society and, inevitably, an intimate of Laing. How Findlay would come to believe that he could make a reality of those dreams of a national portrait gallery, which had been pursued fitfully for almost a century, is unclear. He is likely, of course, to have read Carlyle's famous letter which the Society had published in its *Proceedings*, and Laing's ideas on the subject must have made a deep impression on him. This could well have been the catalyst for the financial offer Findlay would soon make – and for the scale of his ultimate commitment to the notion of a gallery of national portraiture.

Other members of this close-knit group were the painters Joseph Noël Paton, Queen's Limner for Scotland and famous for his Oberon and Titania fairy pictures, and William Fettes Douglas, a member of the Royal Scottish Academy since 1854 and its President when Findlay made his offer. He was also a trustee on the Board of Manufactures. Paton had joined the Society as early as 1859, but Douglas did not become a Fellow until 1878, when he became briefly, and rather surprisingly, one of the curators of the Society of Antiquaries' Museum. His membership of the Society more or less coincided with Laing's death, but they must have been on friendly terms long before then, for he had painted a portrait of Laing, surrounded by the documents and works of art that meant so much to him, for the Royal Scottish Academy in 1862 [8]. Fettes Douglas seems also to have been on particularly close terms with John Ritchie Findlay, and it was he who produced the letter of 7 December 1882, from Findlay to himself, that would come to be seen as the second of the two founding 'charters' of the Scottish National Portrait Gallery.

In measured terms, for he was probably repeating arguments he had already read or heard, Findlay states: 'It has often been remarked of Scotland that no modern country of like limited area and population has produced so many men of far more than local eminence in literature, science, art, and arms; yet Scotland has no National Portrait Gallery. It seems natural and fitting that the Board of Trustees, as custodians of the existing Gallery of Painting and Sculpture and as representatives of Government in such matters in Scotland, should take the initiative in any movement that may be made towards supplying this desideratum.' Like the good businessman he was, he then turned to the financial aspects of what he was proposing.

Findlay's initial offer was of £10,000 towards 'an undertaking' which he thought could be realised for around £40,000 or £50,000. The remaining sums could come, he believed, from the Board of Manufactures (£10,000), a public appeal (£10,000), and the government. He asked Fettes Douglas to convey his offer to the Board, with

the proviso that his anonymity must be preserved. This condition would be kept religiously. However, his dream that the public and the government would contribute in any substantial way was to remain only that. The government matched his initial offer with an endowment of £10,000, but in the end he contributed virtually the remainder of the cost himself.

8 *David Laing*
by William Fettes
Douglas, 1862
Transferred from
the Scottish National
Gallery to the Portrait
Gallery in 1964,
P G 2041

THE MAIN PLAYERS

Throughout the period between 1882, the year in which the Scottish National Portrait Gallery can be said to have come into being, and 1906, when the embellishment of its new building was completed, a small number of names occur again and again in the records of how the project was brought to fruition [9–14]. First among these, of course, was John Ritchie Findlay. Almost as important as Findlay was the chosen architect Robert Rowand Anderson, architect to the Board of Manufactures and one of the most versatile and prolific practitioners of the time. Among the six members of a committee of the Board of Manufactures appointed to oversee the erection of the building were the two artists, Noël Paton and Fettes Douglas. Of the two, Fettes Douglas was the more active and opinionated, and was a conduit to Findlay on how the donor viewed progress. The four other members

were Arthur Halkett, a long-retired soldier; Lord Kinnear, a judge expert in land matters; John Inglis, Lord Glencorse, at the time Lord Justice General (as an advocate, he had successfully defended Madeleine Smith in a notorious murder trial); and the 9th Marquess of Lothian, Schomberg Henry Kerr. Of these, Lord Lothian was by far the most active, and as Secretary for Scotland in Parliament had wide-ranging influence.

Although not a member of this committee there was another major player in these years, John Crichton-Stuart, 3rd Marquess of Bute. A dedicated medievalist and romantic, Lord Bute had become acquainted with Robert Rowand Anderson in 1871 through their membership of the Society of Antiquaries of Scotland. They would remain intimate over the next thirty years, Lord Bute becoming a major patron in a variety of buildings, but particularly in the creation of his great palace, Mount Stuart, on the Isle of Bute, which was erected in the years 1880 to 1885. The building of the Portrait Gallery thus followed close on the heels of Mount Stuart, with which it has much in common, though the latter is far more lavishly decorated, the result of Lord Bute's extraordinary wealth.

In addition to these, another small group of men (inevitably men) loom large in the earliest part of the story: Alexander Inglis, Secretary to the Board of Manufactures; John Miller Gray, banker and aesthete who became the first Curator of the Portrait Gallery; and James Caw, who succeeded him and would go on to play a major role as Director of the National Galleries of Scotland from 1907.

Clockwise from top left:

9 *Sir Joseph Noël Paton* by W. Graham Boss
Presented by the artist, PG 1701

10 *Sir William Fettes Douglas* by W. Graham Boss
Presented by the artist, PG 1700

11 *Sir Robert Rowand Anderson* by W. Graham Boss
Presented by the artist, PG 1699

12 *Schomberg Henry Kerr, 9th Marquess of Lothian* by W. Graham Boss
Presented by the artist, PG 1714

13 *John Patrick Crichton-Stuart, 3rd Marquess of Bute* by W. Graham Boss
Presented by the artist, PG 1710

14 *John Ritchie Findlay* by W. Graham Boss
Presented by the artist, PG 1702

CHAPTER TWO

THE VISION OF
JOHN RITCHIE FINDLAY

IF there is one hero in the early history of the Scottish National Portrait Gallery it is John Ritchie Findlay [15]. Yet such was his modesty that he would have demurred at the notion and would no doubt have preferred to have gone on being called the anonymous donor, if that had been practical. But his role certainly was heroic, not only in the degree of his munificence but in his day-to-day commitment to the project and the energy with which he drove it forward. He was clear what he wanted, and made it plain without ever being aggressive.

Until the new building was opened on 15 July 1889, and its decoration completed in the years that followed, the whole conception moved forward to Findlay's tune. He balanced his overwhelming dedication to the notion of a Portrait Gallery against what he also saw as his obligations to the Society of Antiquaries of Scotland, on whose Council he served and whose Secretary he was from 1882 to 1888. In some of the documentation of the period, he shows himself consistently to be worried that he had actually prejudiced the interests of the Society in finding a home for its collections, which were still squeezed chaotically into the Royal Institution building, along with the Board of Manufactures' art school (which was also bursting at the seams due to the number of women who wanted to study there) and another tenant, the Royal Society of Edinburgh. It was this sense of obligation that would in the end lead to his agreement to allow the Society to have premises in his Portrait Gallery, although it compromised his original vision and led to more than a century of sometimes uneasy cohabitation.

Findlay's initial offer of £10,000 to 'set on foot' a National Portrait Gallery, made on 7 December 1882 in his letter to Fettes Douglas, included a number of conditions: that he, as donor, should remain anonymous; that the Board should seek a further £10,000 from a public appeal; and that he would make his money available if progress was made within six months. This latter condition is the first clear indication of the urgency that Findlay would bring to the project. Although progress was rapid initially, a number of factors caused delay. The trustees of the Board of Manufactures had to continually defer to the Treasury in London from where most of their funding came. There was the vexed question of finding adequate accommodation for the Society of Antiquaries, which was peculiarly demanding concerning its needs, and the whole business of creating what the Treasury was soon referring to as 'the Scottish Historical Portrait Gallery' was an entirely new one to those involved.

At the beginning there was no clear intention to erect a new building and the Treasury, as might be expected, and despite Findlay's generosity, simply looked at the possibility of allocating the various bodies they had to deal with to new places in existing buildings. Leonard Courtney, Financial Secretary to the Treasury, who

15 *John Ritchie Findlay* by Thomas Rodger
PGP 38.1

loomed large in the proceedings, wrote to the Board suggesting that 'room might be found' in the Royal Institution building at the Mound for the new Portrait Gallery. Since the Portrait Gallery would thus be sharing that building with the trustees' art school, and since the adjacent building to the south already housed both the Scottish National Gallery and the Royal Scottish Academy, the Mound would become what the Treasury frequently called an 'art centre' – a concept which has survived to the present day though in a rather different form. To achieve this, the Treasury was pressing the Society of Antiquaries to relocate from the Royal Institution building to what was then known as the Museum of Science and Art in Chambers Street [16]. This move would not be a merger, and so that the Society's distinct identity would be maintained they were offered an 'unbroken wall' between their rooms and the rest of the building. However, as Lord Glencorse would remark with understatement at the opening of the Portrait Gallery in 1889, the Society was 'somewhat hard to please' and rejected the space offered as inadequate.

In the meantime, the still-anonymous donor's initial £10,000 had been matched by the Treasury, and Findlay quickly turned his attention towards the contents of the new Gallery and how it should be curated. But, at the same time he grew frustrated by the lack of 'practical steps' towards his dream, as he explained in a letter to Fettes Douglas on 28 November 1883: 'Now I certainly never intended that

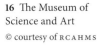

16 The Museum of Science and Art

© courtesy of RCAHMS

the money should be laid up in a napkin, or even put out to usury by the Board.'

Although Findlay had always emphasised that it was a portrait gallery he had set out to create, he remained sensitive to the needs of the Society of Antiquaries, and felt quite strongly that they should be given 'better accommodation' than 'they are to obtain in the new wing of the Industrial Museum'. Such was his feeling that he had prejudiced their need for better premises than those they presently occupied in the Royal Institution building, that by the spring of 1884 he had either conceived the idea, or been persuaded, that the Museum of Antiquities should be housed in the same building as the Portrait Gallery. To that end he wrote to Fettes Douglas (who passed on his letter to Alexander Inglis, Secretary to the Board, on 28 April) that he was 'prepared to place a further sum of money at the disposal of the Board' provided that 'the whole sum be at once devoted to the erection of an adequate edifice' and that 'a suitable and isolated site be provided by the Government, by the City of Edinburgh, by the Board of Trustees or by any or all of these bodies jointly …' The sum he proposed to offer was £15,000, but by the time it was discussed at a special meeting of the Board called on 11 June 1884, the amount had increased to £20,000. This sum was now offered unambiguously for the accommodation 'both of the National Portrait Gallery, and of the Museum of Antiquities'. There were two conditions: there must be practical action before 1 September of the following year; and the money was to be spent either on a new building, or, if an existing building was bought (and that remained a possibility at this time), the money could be spent on both its purchase and conversion. No part of the £20,000 was to be spent on acquiring a site. The memorandum concerning this extraordinary offer that was sent to the Treasury two days later pointed out that the proposed arrangement would allow the Board to expand their art school within the Royal Institution. All of this was music to the ears of the Treasury, who saw the problems of their art policies in Scotland being solved without much effort or major public expenditure.

The same memorandum went on to note that a suitable site for a new building was already on the market. It measured 262 × 70 feet and was 'quite isolated, and not in contact with any other buildings'. (This was strictly correct, but misleading, as the proximity of other buildings, as will be seen, would create hazards that were not entirely eliminated until the 1980s.) The site, a vacant lot to the north of what had been the private gardens on that side of St Andrew Square, was available for £7,500. The Board offered £2,500 towards its purchase, taken from money it had set aside for an extension of their art school. It was also the Board's belief that a suitable building could be created for £20,000 because of the 'present low rate of wages in the building trade'. The Treasury readily found the money to complete the purchase but stressed that no further 'grant from Public Funds towards the cost of Building will be made to this Board'.

The Board, however, made one further request to the Treasury on 14 July and that was to ask if it would pay for the 'fitting up' of the part of the building that would be dedicated to the Museum of Antiquities, as they had already undertaken to defray this cost if the Museum had gone to the Museum of Science and Art. Four

Board of Manufactures
SKETCH PLANS
FOR
...tion of Portrait Gallery
AND
Museum of Antiquities

Front Elevation

17 One of the early sketch plans for the National Portrait Gallery and the Museum of Antiquities by Robert Rowand Anderson

Edinburgh University Library, Special Collections Department

days later Leonard Courtney agreed to this. Findlay had now seen major progress towards his goal well before his deadline.

THE ARCHITECT

It seemed plain sailing after the Board's architect, Robert Rowand Anderson, was appointed in 1884 to design the new building [17]. Anderson, a friend of Findlay's, had by this time almost reached the pinnacle of his success in a career that saw relatively few of the setbacks usually attendant on his profession. As a young man he had started to train as a lawyer, but had switched to architecture by 1853 when he attended classes at the trustee's art school. After working in the practice of John Lessels in Edinburgh he had worked in the office of the Gothic revivalist, George Gilbert Scott, in London. During 1859 he had made a prolonged tour of France and Italy, primarily to study secular buildings of the thirteenth and fourteenth centuries, through both sketching and photography. He published these studies in 1868 in *The Domestic and Street Architecture of France and Italy* and some of the illustrations in that book, for example those of the Maison du Grand Veneur in Cordes and the Place Champollion in Figeac, make clear where some of his inspiration for the Portrait Gallery commission would come from. All the buildings share a predilection for arcades of large, bluntly pointed arches at street level and clusters of twinned windows at higher levels, all set against quite large areas of blank wall.

The early success of his independent practice in Edinburgh was founded on work for the Scottish Episcopal Church, which was erecting many new church buildings during the 1860s. The following decade saw the erection of his vast, aisleless church for the Catholic Apostolic Church in London Road in Edinburgh, designed in a neo-Norman style that demonstrates Anderson's easy confidence in using whatever forms were demanded of him. By the time he was given the Portrait Gallery commission in 1884, he had either completed, or was still working on, an astonishing array of major commissions: the Medical School for the University of Edinburgh in an Italian Renaissance style (begun in 1878 but not completed until 1886); the office block at Central Station in Glasgow which has Flemish elements (also begun in 1878 and converted, by Anderson, to a hotel between 1880 and 1883); the Conservative Club in Princes Street in Edinburgh, a kind of Italian palazzo (1882–4); and, most interestingly because of the comparisons that can be made with the Portrait Gallery, Mount Stuart on the Isle of Bute, the designs of which, for John Crichton-Stuart, the 3rd Marquess of Bute, he had started working on in 1879 [18].

Anderson, who had a profound interest in the archaeology of buildings, had joined the Society of Antiquaries in 1871 and it was there that he got to know Lord Bute, and other establishment figures like the Earl of Northesk, William Forbes Skene and the Marquess of Lothian. The latter, like Bute, would be fruitful (sometimes too fruitful for Anderson) of suggestions for the embellishment of the Portrait Gallery as building was in progress. Anderson and Bute had a happy rapport over Mount Stuart, the great 'island palace' that was completed the year after Anderson started work on the Portrait Gallery plans. The similarities between

18 Mount Stuart, 1906
© RCAHMS (Henry Bedford Lemere Collection)

19 Interior of Mount Stuart showing staircase and celestial ceiling, 1906
© RCAHMS (Henry Bedford Lemere Collection)

the two buildings are considerable, but Mount Stuart's interior is far more lavish [19]. Unlike the Portrait Gallery it was lit by electricity internally, but it was built using the same red Corsehill sandstone from Dumfriesshire.

Apart from his experience in using this material at Mount Stuart, there is no obvious reason why something so foreign to Edinburgh's cityscape should have been chosen – and its friability in Edinburgh's sooty atmosphere would soon cause problems that proved to be long term. Was this startling difference in colour an early example of an architect seeking the 'shock and awe' effect which is now so often the aim of contemporary museum design? Was Anderson's rich, neo-thirteenth-century French Gothic detailing, so unlike the plain, rectilinear late Georgian buildings of Edinburgh's New Town that surrounded the Portrait Gallery, a deliberate statement of difference – of the same kind if not the same degree, that marks Frank Gehry's sleek, unfolding museum in Bilbao?

THE FIRST CURATOR

At the same time as John Ritchie Findlay was forcing the pace of the building project, he also turned his mind to the question of how the nascent collection should be curated. His exchanges with the Board also draw a sharp, even amusing, contrast with how such a matter would be approached today. In the same letter in which Findlay had bemoaned the lack of practical steps towards using his money

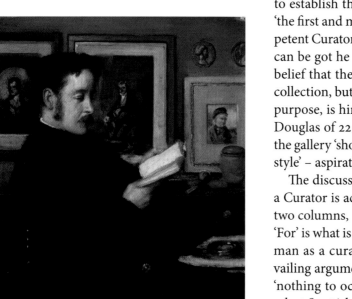

to establish the Gallery, he went so far as to say that 'the first and most important step is to appoint a competent Curator for the proposed Gallery. If such a man can be got he cannot be too soon in harness ….' His belief that the gallery should be more than simply a collection, but should also have some kind of didactic purpose, is hinted at in a slightly later letter to Fettes Douglas of 22 December 1883 where he remarks that the gallery 'should be started in a popular and effective style' – aspirations that have a contemporary ring.

The discussion document that sets out to clarify if a Curator is actually necessary is starkly divided into two columns, 'Points For' and 'Points Against'. Under 'For' is what is evidently Findlay's contribution: 'Good man as a curator is available (cheap).' The countervailing argument was that the 'New Man' would have 'nothing to occupy him sufficiently… Anyone could select Scottish portraits [from the Watson Bequest, a group of material already bequeathed by a bookseller, William Finlay Watson, or from the forthcoming loan

20 *John Miller Gray* by Patrick William Adam, 1885
Bequeathed by the sitter in 1894, PG 1226

exhibition of Scottish National Portraits to be mounted in June 1884] … therefore only a new Clerk would be required.' Not surprisingly, Findlay got his way and on 26 February 1884 the *Courant* newspaper was able to announce the appointment of John Miller Gray [20]. This first Curator was a highly cultivated antiquarian and aesthete (the English art critic, Walter Pater was one of his referees), a former bank employee and of not very robust health. He did not, of course, at this stage have a Gallery to run, and his first task was to organise the 1884 loan exhibition (of more than 600 items) which had the aim, as Gray remarks in his introduction to the catalogue, of 'interesting the public in the subject of Portraiture generally', an exercise that was mounted 'in anticipation of the opening of the permanent Scottish National Portrait Gallery'.

THE NEW BUILDING

The planning and construction of the Gallery proceeded quite quickly, with Anderson submitting several plans to the Board of Manufactures on 24 October 1884; these were remitted to a committee, which reported to the Board three weeks later. The exterior of the building would present few problems, and there was little discussion of the functionality of its interior. There were, however, two areas of contention: the allocation of space between the two institutions that were to inhabit it; and the decoration of both the exterior and the interior. The space problem had to be, and was, solved quite quickly, but the decoration and the discussions which attended it continued over a number of years.

The committee appear to have considered three plans, but their overriding aim was practical, and political, and that was to choose something that could be built for £20,000, and to fulfil the promise made to the Treasury to provide the Museum of Antiquities with very substantial space. The committee's report makes it quite clear that the two collections were to be divided by the 'eastern wall of the central block'. All the space to the east, including a separate staircase, was to be exclusively for the Society's Museum, while the Great Hall, its ambulatory and the galleries to the west, also including a separate staircase, were to be reserved for the Portrait Gallery. This arrangement gave 8,881 square feet to the Gallery and 10,396 square feet to the Museum. It is not easy to understand these figures unless the basement on the Museum side of the building is taken into account – there was to be no basement in the Gallery wing. In whatever way these figures are understood, the committee set out to justify the discrepancy by pointing out that the Society of Antiquaries, who had only 3,264 square feet in the Royal Institution building, had requested 12,630 square feet if they were to be moved to Chambers Street. The Treasury had responded to this demand by offering them 8,465 square feet at Chambers Street, but once more the Society of Antiquaries had dug their heels in and rejected the offer on the grounds that the space would not allow for further expansion.

It was against this background that the committee bent over backwards to justify what it had done and felt it necessary 'to direct the special attention of the Board to the fact that the Donor did not give the Board any information on his desires in regard to the allocation of the space in the proposed new building to the two Institutions until after all the arrangements were concluded between Board and the Treasury, with the entire approval of the Donor.' Given Findlay's generosity and the Board's awareness that his grand plan had been to create a National Portrait

Gallery and nothing else, it is a curiously ungracious argument. It was presumably this that moved Fettes Douglas to write a couple of weeks later to Alexander Inglis, that if 'the Board had intimated to him [that is, the donor, after his second gift of £20,000] that in the new Building the Antiquarians were to have the Chief place and consideration he would never have placed the money at their disposal'. He went on to reiterate Findlay's view that everything should be done in the design of the building 'to avoid all possibility of its [the Portrait Gallery] being confounded in the mind or eye of the public with any other Institution accommodated in the same building'. It remains unclear how this issue was resolved, but the much put-upon Findlay again appears to have provided the solution. A partly illegible draft minute contains phrases such as 'fresh instance of the anonymous Donor's generosity' and 'prospect of his great and patriotic design being brought to an … & satisfactory completion.' To emphasise the Board's concern, a copy of the minute was to be transmitted to the donor by the Lord Justice General. The matter was finally laid to rest at a Board meeting on 8 January 1885 when it was noted that because of the donor's 'auspicious intervention at a somewhat embarrassing crisis, difficulties have been overcome'.

Anderson's original design underwent few major changes. He had proposed quite massive round towers embedded at the four corners, but Findlay did not like these, mainly because they wasted internal space. After his intervention, these were replaced by the present less massive octagonal section turrets, those at the

21 Drawing showing the building with the tourelles at each end of the central block
Edinburgh University Library, Special Collections Department

22 Drawing with amendments to the original plan
Edinburgh University Library, Special Collections Department

23 Drawing of the final design showing the existing turrets
Edinburgh University Library, Special Collections Department

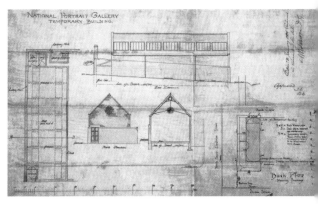

24 Sketch of the temporary gallery by Sir George Scharf, 1887

25 Drawing of the temporary gallery by Robert Rowand Anderson
Edinburgh City Archives

north-west and south-east containing narrow spiral staircases [21–3]. While the west gable end (at this time facing a narrow strip of garden which was later built on) was to remain plain, an apsidal form was initially intended in the centre of the east gable facing onto North St Andrew Street. This quite striking feature was dropped and the elaborate fenestration of the façade at first floor level simply wrapped round the building at this point, but interrupted by a large central niche for sculpture (to be filled in 1896 with the group of Mary, Queen of Scots with William Maitland of Lethington and John Lesley).

Even before building work was underway, a modest temporary building was erected on the eastern perimeter of the site. By a nice irony, the principal evidence of what this little building looked like is a pencil sketch made on 20 August 1887 by the Director of the London Portrait Gallery, George Scharf [24]. Scharf, still seeking a home for his own gallery, must have been intrigued to see what was happening in Edinburgh and was no doubt impressed by the incomplete new building and what it promised. It is highly likely that it was what was going on in Edinburgh that encouraged another donor, William Henry Alexander, to offer to pay for a dedicated building for the London National Portrait Gallery in May 1889, a project that would be completed in 1896.

Scharf's drawing of the temporary Scottish National Portrait Gallery shows a basic, brick building with a stone frontage to Queen Street. The slated roof was sliced from back to front on both slopes by glass skylights. Recent research has unearthed Anderson's drawing for the building in the archives of the City of Edinburgh, dated 19 December 1884, which attests to the accuracy of Scharf's sketch [25]. Before this building had gone up, Anderson had toyed with the idea of erecting an iron building on the site, for on 18 September 1884 he received a quote from a London firm, J. Humphrey of Hyde Park, to erect such 'a picture gallery, the price of which would be if lined &c complete £340 …' This notion was presumably dropped as being insufficiently grand, but what is made clear by the date of Humphrey's quote is that the temporary home was conceived not only before work had begun on the building but even before the final plans had been accepted – almost certainly another indication of Findlay's urge to get things moving.

As Scharf's drawing shows, the Portrait Gallery building did not rise in a uniform manner, for the bricked-up, temporary gable indicates that work had stopped before the addition of the transverse rooms and the two towers where the temporary building still stood. Early architectural drawings by Anderson show that initially the south-west quarter of the great rectangle, that is, the part bounded by the Portrait Gallery staircase and the galleries in the front half of the building, was not to be built immediately in order to reduce costs. Early in 1886, however, Findlay noticed that the central wall running the length of the first-floor gallery on the Museum's side had been built with open arches, while the same wall in the Portrait Gallery half of the building was unbroken – it was currently acting as an exterior wall because the south-western section had yet to be built. By this time the donor seems to have become committed to the notion of complete symmetry between the two institutions, and the only way to achieve that was to open up arches in the Portrait Gallery's wall and complete the missing part of the building. He offered £2,500 for this purpose and the work went ahead. At the beginning of 1887 Findlay made his final, major intervention, when it was agreed to build the transverse wings at either end of the building. For his perfectionism, the donor now found himself committing a further £12,000. This seems to bring the cost to himself of his vision to build a Scottish National Portrait Gallery to £44,500. Findlay had also given £500 towards the cost of the loan exhibition of portraits of 1884 in the Scottish National Gallery, so that by the time the Scottish National Portrait Gallery was opened by the Marquess of Lothian in 1889, the anonymous donor, whose identity was revealed to the few who did not already know it during the crowded opening ceremony, had spent some £45,000. However, *The Scotsman* newspaper report of the ceremony quotes a figure of 'little less than £50,000', a similar figure to that quoted in an article in the *The Art Journal* in January 1890, almost certainly contributed by J.M. Gray. The likely explanation of the discrepancy is that Findlay paid the full estimated cost of the two end sections, some £5,000, rather than the £2,500 he had offered. It was all a familiar, and unfinished, story.

The building that Rowand Anderson, and Findlay, had erected was essentially one of stone, brick and malleable iron, and of an overall simplicity despite its elaborate exterior [26–31]. Yet, as a building and despite its architectural magnificence, it was to have a troubled history for much of the succeeding century – trouble that stemmed from a variety of factors which included what came to be seen as inadequacies in some of its structural features, the instability of the red Corsehill sandstone that Anderson claimed had proved itself impervious to London's polluted atmosphere, and the events of the terrible twentieth century which led to long periods when the building had to be used for other purposes. When the closures due to two world wars are aggregated with those necessitated by bringing the safety of the building up to modern standards, it is quite astonishing that in the years prior to 1949 the Portrait Gallery was unable to fulfil its public function for over a third of the time.

When the Portrait Gallery opened to the public in 1889 (the Museum of Antiquities would follow in 1891) the collection was confined to the first-floor gallery – usually referred to as two galleries, but virtually one because of the opening

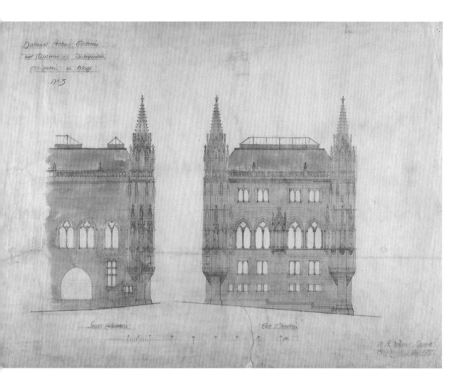

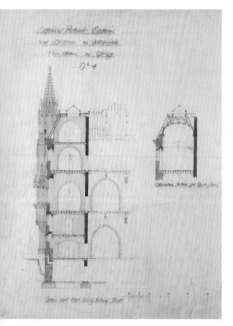

Clockwise from top left:

26 East and part of the south elevation of the building
Edinburgh University Library, Special Collections Department

27 Detail of the spire
Edinburgh University Library, Special Collections Department

28 Window detail
Edinburgh University Library, Special Collections Department

29 Part section of the building
Edinburgh University Library, Special Collections Department

up of the dividing wall that Findlay had insisted on. The ground-floor galleries were to be occupied from 1890 by another cuckoo in the nest, the Royal Geographical Society, though Findlay seemed quite happy with this, and what was called a Lecture Hall. The Society was to remain there until 1907 when it was displaced by the recently established Board of Trustees for the National Galleries of Scotland moving their offices into the west wing, at both ground and mezzanine level, where the Secretary to the Board had a separate office at the foot of the spiral staircase – an impediment to easy movement within the building that would remain in place for many years. The Board also took as their own the little doorway on the north wall of this wing that had previously given access to special exhibitions by outside bodies on the ground floor – for example, an exhibition of architectural photographs from New York's Brooklyn Museum in 1905.

THE LATER LIFE OF THE BUILDING

As early as 1912 it had dawned on the Board that the building was insufficiently fire-resistant. They informed the Council of the Society of Antiquaries of the need to replace the existing floors throughout the building and suggested that half should be done at a time, starting with the Museum of Antiquities. This would mean shifting the Museum's collection into the Portrait Gallery part of the building, so that the floors and roof could be reconstructed in concrete and the wrought iron beams replaced with steel joists. The matchboarding on the walls would be stripped out and the pine floorboards would be replaced with parquet flooring. The Society of Antiquaries' principal concern seems to have been about the cost of moving their collections. In the event, however, the principal architect in the Office of Works, William Thomas Oldrieve, had to write to Robert Wood, the new Secretary to the Board of Trustees for the National Galleries of Scotland, that the Treasury had 'disallowed the provision made in this office for expenditure

30 *Scottish National Portrait Gallery Exterior* by Thomas Crawford Hamilton, 1890

Given by J. Kent Richardson in 1944, PG 1760a

31 *Scottish National Portrait Gallery Interior* by Thomas Crawford Hamilton, 1890

Given by J. Kent Richardson in 1944, PG 1760b

during the financial year, 1913–14, for fireproofing the floors, etc. ...' The 'etc.' here refers to the heating system in the building which Oldrieve also argued should be replaced, a view supported by Lionel Earle of the Office of Works in London who believed that it was in a dangerous condition. Approval was eventually given the following year, however, for a slightly reduced scheme costing some £15,375, and Wood posted the ominous information that 'The Scottish National Portrait Gallery will be closed from Thursday, 12th March, until further notice'.

World war and economic recession followed, and there seemed no prospect of carrying out similar work in the Portrait Gallery's part of the building. Indeed, the work in the Museum had been suspended in 1916–17 and was not completed until 1919–20. In the meantime, the Portrait Gallery suffered as many as three further invasions. As early as March 1916 the Ancient Monuments Commission requested, and was granted, permission to store their books and maps in the central gallery on the top floor. Later, the Ministry of Pensions occupied the ground floor and the Timber Supply Department took up residence in the first floor and other parts of the building. They, however, had moved out by the end of 1919, by which time James Caw, the Director of the National Galleries of Scotland (at this time he also styled himself Director of the Portrait Gallery) was making representations for the remainder of the work to be completed. He had the support of the Under Secretary of State, but the Treasury was deaf to their appeals. He had also made direct contact with John Stirling Maxwell, at the Board of Trade, who was responsible for the Timber Supply Department, and this seems to have hastened that department's removal.

By the spring of 1921, the Treasury was still refusing to sanction work – and still referring to the effects of the war. This time the trustees played the public opinion card, stressing the 'numerous enquiries [that] are addressed daily to the doorkeeper of the Building as to when the place will be re-opened'. It had no effect, and in August the Office of Works (in Westminster) had to inform the Scottish Office (in Whitehall) that their provision in draft estimates for completing the fireproofing of the building had been deleted by the Treasury: 'In face of the present overwhelming pressure for economy, it seems very doubtful whether further progress can be made with the work for several years.' There is a sense here of a great distance, not entirely of miles, between Edinburgh and London, and the question might be asked if such a curious state of affairs would have been allowed to persist in a national museum in the latter city. Despite this impasse, the trustees were determined to re-open, even with an old steam-heating system where it was 'not uncommon during the winter months to find the glass of pictures steamed, and the surface of unglazed pictures wet with condensed moisture'. Some money was forthcoming for cleaning and redecoration, and the Portrait Gallery re-opened on 12 April 1922 after a closure of more than seven years.

As for the necessary fireproofing, Fate (or was it History, with her gilded halo, still atop the building?) was about to intervene. Around nine o'clock on the night of 7 January 1929 a fire started in a large building across the narrow lane which separated the Portrait Gallery from the north side of St Andrew Square. The building

32 The fire in the former Tolbooth Free Church, 7 January 1929
National Library of Scotland

33 Queen Mary visiting the re-opened building on 4 July 1934, accompanied by Hew Dalrymple and Stanley Cursiter
SNPG Reference Section

was a former church, the Tolbooth Free Church, erected in 1857, but by this time owned by the Bank of Scotland and used each morning as a clearing house [32]. As Robert Moncrieff, the new Secretary to the Board of Trustees, reported to the Under Secretary of State, 'within an hour only the four walls remained'. Two firemen had been positioned on the roof of the Portrait Gallery to hose down sparks, and Moncrieff had now armed himself with a letter from Edinburgh's fire-master who had no doubt that unless this action had been taken the roof would have caught fire. Moncrieff also stressed that similar dangers remained: next door to the destroyed building, Jenners department store had a van lock-up and a petrol tank; and only four feet from the western gable of the building were 'two lightly constructed shops, wood-lined and having a roof covered with zinc'.

The situation was obviously dire and action was almost immediate, by Treasury standards. By February of the following year they were actually insisting that 'the fireproofing should be comprehensive', the work being estimated at £15,000. During the same discussions, the question of inserting a lift in the narrow 'chase', included in the museum part of the building for that purpose, was raised. The Under Secretary of State initially doubted the utility of such a device, however, and demurred at the cost of a lift attendant, who would take up valuable space within its narrow confines. Both Moncrieff and John Ritchie Findlay (son of the donor) were able to persuade him that the public were now quite capable of using automatic lifts unsupervised. Findlay also offered the £950 which was still lying in his father's decoration fund – and the lift was in due course installed by the Medways Safety Lift Company for £828.19s.8d.

So, once again, early in 1931 the Portrait Gallery was closed to the public. During this period of major reconstruction, however, a selection of portraits was kept on view in the central gallery on the top floor; and deep in what was virtually a building site the opportunity was taken to reorganise the collections of engravings, drawings and record photographs which were carefully indexed. This material was established in a Print Room which would eventually be accessible to visitors.

Fireproofing completed, the reopening of the building was marked by a visit on 4 July 1934 by Queen Mary who was conducted round the building by the Chairman of the Trustees for the National Galleries of Scotland, Hew Dalrymple, someone who over the years contributed a great deal to the record-keeping function of the Portrait Gallery [33]. When the queen made her way back to Holyroodhouse, the press noticed that she broke her short journey at Dalrymple's house in Regent Terrace in order 'to view his collection'.

A period of calm and consolidation in the history of the Portrait Gallery followed, but the times were ominous. The approaching cataclysm is illustrated in a very mundane way by a small, stamped envelope in the archive. Returned heavily annotated by the Post Office – 'Gone Away', 'not known here', 'Not Known at above address' – it had contained an invitation to the Portrait Gallery's jubilee party on 14 July 1939. The intended recipient, at a London address, was the former Principal of the Heriot-Watt College in Edinburgh, Arthur Pillans Laurie. Laurie was a chemist with an international reputation and a particular interest in artists' materials and the history of their techniques. He had published many books on the subject, including the classic, *The Painter's Methods and Materials*. But Laurie happened to be a Nazi sympathiser, an enthusiastic attender of Nuremberg rallies, and had just published a book in Berlin, *The Case for Germany*, dedicated to Hitler – all of which was presumably unknown to the then Keeper of the Gallery, Archibald Haswell Miller. In the circumstances, it is hardly surprising that the Post Office had failed to find him. The party, a 'buffet tea' for 'a representative company' of over 300 guests, provided by that vanished Edinburgh institution, McVities, was addressed by the Secretary of State for Scotland, John Colville, and it now seems an amusing reflection of how closely the National Galleries of Scotland were still tied to government that he had to authorise the exceptional expenditure of £30 on the tea and cakes.

It was the end of an era. The 'war emergency', much discussed by the trustees throughout 1939, became a reality two months later and yet again the Portrait Gallery had to close. The building was taken over by the Central National Registration Office, who occupied the ground-floor gallery and parts of the first and upper floors, and the pictures were despatched to a number of houses in the Borders – initially Manderston House, Winton Castle, Fairnilee House, Leithen Lodge, Glenormiston, The Glen and, later, Tweedknowe near Selkirk. Here they languished in less than ideal conditions, each house guarded by a single attendant, furnished in due course with a stirrup-pump.

The building, however, was not entirely abandoned. The Print Room remained intact and was cared for by 'a first class attendant', a Mr Hutton. In addition, towards the end of 1940, the trustees appointed a 'technical officer' to carry out conservation work on the collections of both the National Gallery and the Portrait

Gallery. Paying initially £4 a week, the post went to someone who would acquire a great reputation in the restoration world, Harry Woolford. By the end of the war he would become Keeper of the Scottish National Gallery and ultimately Head of the Conservation Department of the National Galleries of Scotland – a department which had its humble beginnings in the attic space of the Portrait Gallery. There was clearly a good deal of life in the building, including the three police constables

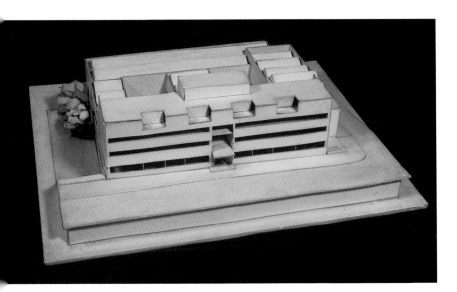

on duty. With bomb damage not difficult to imagine, the glass lay-lights in the two upper long galleries were taken down, and a wire-mesh screen erected under the great cupola in the central gallery on the top floor.

The possibility of defeat in the war seems never to have been an issue for the trustees and, prompted again and again by Stanley Cursiter, who had become Director of the National Galleries of Scotland in 1937, they were soon planning for its aftermath [35]. The lack of adequate storage for both the Portrait Gallery and the National Gallery was of concern, and the notion of a new building for the Museum of Antiquities was aired. Plans were produced by the architect Alan Reiach for a 'Gallery of Modern Art' on the site of York Buildings, immediately across Queen Street from the Portrait Gallery [34]. More immediately, the trustees were anxious to get the two galleries open to the public once more when hostilities ceased. Although its collection had been dispersed, the National Gallery had remained open throughout the war as the venue for a vast array of exhibitions – sometimes a new one every month, ranging from the Scottish Colourists to war propaganda to the work of Chinese schoolchildren – and was able to return to its proper use quite quickly when the war ended. It would be a different matter, however, for the Portrait Gallery.

As early as October 1944, the Board of Trustees, still led by Hew Dalrymple, were pressing the Ministry of Works 'to secure accommodation elsewhere [for the

34 Model of a proposed Gallery of Modern Art for Scotland by Alan Reiach
Scottish National Gallery of Modern Art,
GMA A60/01

35 *Stanley Cursiter* by Lida Moser, 1949
Purchased in 1984,
PGP 43.11

National Registration Office] so that the Portrait Gallery building can resume its normal functions as early as possible when the European War ceases'. It was not to be. Complaints about continued occupation by the Registration Office became a litany that lasted for the next five years, sometimes in the form of direct appeals by the Chairman of the Trustees (now Lord Linlithgow, who had succeeded Hew Dalrymple in January 1945) to the Secretary of State or the Minister of Works. A number of solutions appeared on the horizon only to fade away. The suggestions are redolent of the times: temporary accommodation to be built at the industrial estate of Sighthill, or the acquisition of a disused hosiery factory in Portobello Road. It was not until January 1949, however, that the Minister of Works, the aptly named Mr Keys, was able to announce that accommodation for the Registration Office had been found in Shandwick Place, in the city's west end, and that he hoped the Portrait Gallery would be vacated by the end of March. This time he kept his word. The few curatorial and technical staff that existed at that time, including Robin Hutchison who had filled the new post of Assistant Keeper the previous August, now moved with some speed – the ground floor was re-hung by 12 May, the two upper galleries by 29 May and the central gallery, or Square Room (as it continued to be called), by 6 June. It was an effort that received hearty congratulations from the trustees.

Throughout this period the exterior of the building posed ever-growing problems. Even longer periods of time would be required to solve them. Rowand Anderson's faith in Corsehill sandstone proved to be misplaced. The earliest reference to a problem with the external stonework is a note to Rowand Anderson in January 1907 from the Clerk of Works Office, stating that expenditure of over £300 had been incurred in the 'renovation and waterproofing of the external hewn stone'. It was also noted that 'the remainder of the carved pinnacles have been carefully examined and renewed where necessary in "Locharbriggs" [another quarry in Dumfriesshire] stone'. In August 1922 a Ministry of Works report noted a series of tests carried out by the company of J. Allen How which had led them to believe that 'the primary cause of flaking was the damp town atmosphere. Moisture penetrating the stone [had] caused the formation of sulphate of lime and the stone was consequently opened up to frost action'. At a more anecdotal level, a diary kept by the Print Room attendant noted that on the night of 15 August 1937 the 'Policeman on duty [this was still the form of overnight security] reported that two more large pieces fell from the N.E. corner of the building'. The 'more' tells its own story.

It was now downhill all the way. In the post-war period, when there was no prospect of proper restoration, a good deal of patching with what was in effect pink cement was carried out by the Department of the Environment. Over time this only made the problem worse. By 1975, a study by the Property Services Agency, part of the Department of the Environment, remarked that the 'opportunity [had] been taken to examine the extent to which restoration of the exterior stonework has become necessary'. No action was taken, and by 1980 the building, in the interests of safety, had been denuded of the crockets on the spires, followed by the spires themselves, and the balustrade at roof level, as well as other parts of the decorative stonework. The building's continuation in this state for a number of years no doubt contributed to the remarks of the then Marquess of Bute, John Crichton-Stuart, a trustee of the National Galleries and Chairman of the Portrait Gallery Advisory Committee, that the Gallery had become a 'cultural slum'.

By the late 1970s, however, the Cockburn Association, in a memorandum to the committee on National Museums and Galleries in Scotland, was able to record its pleasure that 'proposals are in hand to restore the exterior of the Queen Street building'. In 1981 the cost of a complete restoration package, to be spread over a ten year period, had been estimated at £1.6 million, and work got underway carving the more elaborate replacement stonework off-site [36–41]. Some of the red sandstone used by the carver, Ian Ketchen, was salvaged from a dismantled railway bridge in Leith. Progress was slow initially and the programme, managed by the Hurd Rolland Partnership, would eventually extend over fifteen years; but from the beginning of 1987 the pace quickened and the Keeper of the time was able to welcome an annual expenditure of £440,000. One of Edinburgh's great buildings was being brought back to life; and by the spring of 1988 the Property Services Agency was able to bask in the warm glow of publicity when the restored statues of William Wallace and Robert the Bruce were returned to their niches.

On 18 January 1994 *The Scotsman* newspaper (ever mindful of Findlay) was able

36 The statue of Robert the Bruce before restoration showing the extensive damage to the stonework

37 The statue of William Wallace being removed for conservation

38 The statue of Robert the Bruce being reinstated

39 One of the new finials for the balustrade

to announce the virtual completion of the programme, but there was a wonderful irony in this, for it coincided with the same newspaper's report of a crowded public meeting the previous evening in Edinburgh College of Art that had been called to protest at plans drawn up by the trustees to close the building and to subsume the Portrait Gallery's historical function in a quite different form of museum, described as a 'Gallery of Scottish Art', in a different location. This was perhaps the most extraordinary episode in the history of the Gallery since its inception, and the serpentine twists and turns of this story and the exact nature of the proposal remain controversial.

The building, its future ultimately assured, and its exterior restored to its former glory, was further enhanced by an act of generosity that echoed John Ritchie Findlay's original gift. In what many saw as a direct reaction to the perceived threat to the Portrait Gallery's future, a charitable foundation, the Dunard Fund, came forward with a proposal to buy the vacant building to the immediate west of the gallery, clear the site, landscape it and rent it to the National Galleries of Scotland for a peppercorn rent of £1 per annum. This site had always been problematic, both in aesthetic terms and as a security and fire hazard. Over the years a number of businesses had occupied the makeshift building but the trustees had showed no inclination to buy it on any of the occasions it had come on the market. The

Dunard Fund appeared more or less out of the blue, when it was once again for sale, this time with planning permission to erect a two storey building in its place. The offer was accepted with alacrity, and a long-standing problem for the Portrait Gallery was solved and a disfigurement that should never have been tolerated in the first place was removed. Rowan trees were planted, the area paved, railings and gates erected and public seating installed, and thus a tiny new oasis was created in the city. Past and present were linked in the only possible way by naming the courtyard Findlay Court.

40 The damaged stone-work on the balustrade

41 The balustrade restored

CHAPTER THREE

THE EMBELLISHMENT
OF THE BUILDING

THE Portrait Gallery building was an emphatic statement of national aspiration, of looking forward on the strength of looking back. It was self-consciously different, yet the utilitarian lay at the root of the decisions on its general structure, however much Findlay's vision was modified, and however much the practicality of these decisions would come to be questioned [42, 43]. Given the Victorian ethos from which its founders could not distance themselves, the very fabric of the structure also had to express their ideals, and their sense of how they valued their own place in time and their understanding of the past. To achieve this complexity the building had to be decorated, though decoration is too loose a term to describe the meanings that these late Victorians wished to see woven into the embodiment of their dream.

SCULPTURE

These aims were realised principally through two traditional forms, sculpture on the exterior of the building and mural painting in the interior. Less emphatically, the sculptural played some role in the interior in carved foliate capitals, gilded and with native animals hidden in them. The term 'sculptural' could also apply to the relationship between these elaborate notes and the plain, but polished red brick of the supporting surfaces of the lower parts of the Great Hall, the two staircases and other parts of the interior. This was an interplay that was later lost when these areas were painted (or covered in boards as happened in the western staircase). These surfaces were to a degree reclaimed in the late 1970s and early 1980s when the paint was removed (with enormous difficulty), but the glazed effect was lost for ever.

The discussions of the nature of this programme of embellishment involved, in addition to Rowand Anderson and Findlay who took the lead, Fettes Douglas, Noël Paton, Lord Bute and Lord Lothian. Their early exchanges seem quite unfocused, inevitably revealing their prejudices, and are often quite amusing. Rowand Anderson and Bute were keen on coats of arms, Findlay much less so, remarking laconically that he himself did not have one. Bute suggested the use of mosaic, something Lothian also had a taste for, but Rowand Anderson, although he might accept it in the interior, was resolutely opposed to its use on the exterior of the central entrance bay where he was certain (probably rightly) that notes of strong colour would disrupt the unity of the façade and were inappropriate with sandstone. Bute, at Findlay's prompting, produced a drawing of a figure of History (though he would have settled for Glory or Fame) to stand on the pinnacle of the entrance bay, and noted that it 'ought to be gilded'. Findlay did not approve, especially of the gilded rays emanating from the figure's head. He had probably

42 View of the Scottish National Portrait Gallery from York Place showing the building before the sculptures had been added

© RCAHMS (Henry Bedford Lemere Collection)

[45]

sensed a religious undertone, for the Catholic Bute, writing to the Secretary of the Board of Manufactures, justifies it by comparing it to 'the image of Liberty enlightening the world, at the entrance of New York harbour … no one has ever taken *her* for a Madonna – notwithstanding Irish rule in New York'. He added that mosaic would cost less than sculpture and referred the Board to the Murano Glass company in St James's Street (London) 'who would tell you all about it in 5 minutes'. Bute, currently creating that complete artwork, Mount Stuart, certainly knew what he was talking about. Nevertheless, Findlay, while 'grateful to his Lordship' for the suggestion that his arms should be included in the scheme, felt his ideas were costly and, he added, 'I am under promise to pay'.

The question of sculptural scenes for the central bay was taken up by Noël Paton (whose advice would be sought on the authenticity of the costume on the statues filling the external niches of the building) but this seems to have re-ignited Findlay's anxieties about his original vision. Writing to Alexander Inglis from Aberlour House, he feared that Noël Paton's suggestions would 'emphasise the Antiquarian side of the Buildings, while it is the Gallery I desire to have specially glorified. We should keep to the Historic, not the Pre-Historic'. Although by this time (August 1890) Findlay had accepted the presence of the Museum of Antiquities in his building, it is a revealing aside. But he had not lost his sense of humour. When the content of these relief panels was under discussion and when Bute at the same time raised the question of representing Findlay by his (non-existent) coat of arms, Findlay suggested that he 'might agree to figure as one of the "boys with a printing press" from which of course copies of *The Scotsman* or *Dispatch* [his two newspapers] would be seen issuing. Nothing would be more appropriate …'

The outcome of these exchanges was a central portal of great textural richness, completed between 1891 and 1893, with the sculptural work carried out by William Birnie Rhind [44]. The entire cost was covered by Findlay. At the pinnacle was Bute's figure of History (lost during a later renovation). Within a pure circle 'inscribed' in the steep pediment is an asymmetrical, pre-Union, royal arms of Scotland derived from a fourteenth-century manuscript. Below this, recessed behind the great upper arch of the portal, Scotia is supported by allegories of Industry and Religion. Acting as a predella at the base of this arch, three high relief panels (where Findlay, jokingly, imagined himself depicted) contain multiple figures enacting the Fine Arts, the Sciences and the Ruder Arts (that is, craftsmanship). Just below this, in the spandrels on either side of the main portal (which matches exactly the upper arch), are roundels containing a male torso of War and a female torso of Peace. Standing on elevated plinths on either side of the door are greater than life-size statues of William Wallace and Robert the Bruce – a potent, if simplified, expression of national sentiment. All of this sculptural work was carved by Birnie Rhind. Finally, recessed within this giant portal, was the actual doorway which echoed it (and matched exactly the first-floor windows), within which was carved the post-Union achievement of Scotland.

Decisions about the twenty-eight statues that fill the niches of the corner towers (but not the one at the south-west), the principal façade and the eastern elevation

43 View of the south-east tower showing the poets, John Barbour (left) by Archibald McFarlane Shannan, William Dunbar (centre) by James Pittendrigh Macgillivray and Gavin Douglas (right) by William Grant Stevenson; statues erected in 1904 and 1899

44 *Entrance to the Scottish National Portrait Gallery* by Adam Alexander Inglis, 1895

PGP 524

45 The centre of the east wall with Mary, Queen of Scots and her courtiers, John Lesley (left) and William Maitland (right) by William Birnie Rhind; group erected in 1896

46 View of the north-east tower showing the surgeon and anatomist, John Hunter (left) and the painter, Sir Henry Raeburn (right) by James Pittendrigh Macgillivray; statues erected in 1906 and 1900

 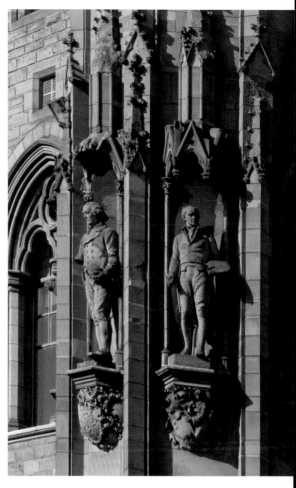

at first-floor level were relatively straightforward. There was, however, a problem of funding, for Findlay had hoped that the statues would be gifted. In the event only eight were, and Findlay had to foot the bill for the remainder. The principal gift was the group of Mary, Queen of Scots and her two courtiers, John Lesley and William Maitland, situated in the large niche in the centre of the east wall of the building, an elevation that Rowand Anderson had been inclined to privilege from his earliest designs [45]. It too was the work of William Birnie Rhind. Its prominence reflects a prevailing romantic view of Scottish history, suggesting that there was no very coherent historical programme in the choice of subject and arrangement of statues. For example, the profoundly significant figure of Mary's son, James VI and I [47], is placed in a relatively inconspicuous position on the main façade. The Mary group, however, contains a strong local echo, for it was donated by a group of Edinburgh ladies calling themselves the 'Queen Mary Statue Committee' to celebrate Findlay's generosity in giving the nation its Portrait Gallery, and also to thank him for his efforts in getting women admitted to the Medical School of the University of Edinburgh.

47 Part of the eastern section of the façade showing James VI and I by David Watson Stevenson; statue erected in 1893

© PMSA (Dianne King)

48 The north-west tower with Admiral Duncan, 1st Viscount Duncan of Camperdown (left) by David Watson Stevenson and Sir Ralph Abercromby (right) by William Birnie Rhind; statues erected in 1902 and 1899

© PMSA (Dianne King)

49 Part of the western section of the façade showing
John Knox by John Hutchison; statue erected in 1902

© PMSA (Dianne King)

The statues were erected between 1899 and 1906. In addition to Birnie Rhind, the sculptors who contributed were Archibald Shannan (one statue), James Pittendrigh Macgillivray (six), William Grant Stevenson (two), his brother David Watson Stevenson (six), John Hutchison (two), Waller Hubert Paton (two) and Henry Snell Gamley (one). They fulfilled Rowand Anderson's belief that sculpture should be integral to a building, but it might be asked if carving them from the same redstone as the building allowed them to be read as individual works of art – it certainly reduced their visibility. Findlay had wanted them identified by name but this was never to be achieved, despite much discussion, and the viewer from street level cannot easily follow this particular exposition of Scottish history. Though the choice of subject might appear eccentric, one decision was clear and that was to exclude those already represented by statuary elsewhere in Edinburgh: hence the omission of Robert Burns (John Flaxman's statue was by this time on loan to the Gallery) and Walter Scott, who had his own vast memorial nearby in Princes Street.

The most coherent group consists of the four early Renaissance poets who have the south-east tower to themselves – John Barbour, William Dunbar, Gavin Douglas and David Lindsay [43]. Otherwise there are some strange gatherings: for example, on the north-east tower the portrait painter Henry Raeburn rubs shoulders with three scientists and a lawyer. It does seem, however, that Raeburn has been carefully positioned on the central face of the pentagonal surface so that he gazes directly, palette and brushes at the ready, towards his old studio across the road in York Place [46]. In the north-west tower, those two great philosophers of the Scottish enlightenment, David Hume and Adam Smith, consort with an admiral and a general [48]. One of those involved in the choice of subject was Major General Robert Murdoch Smith, Director of the Museum of Science and Art, who suggested dropping Dunbar and Hume from Rowand Anderson's list and substituting Thomas Carlyle and Adam Smith. It is not entirely clear why Murdoch Smith was asked for his views, as the Museum of Science and Art had failed to provide the Museum of Antiquities with a home. Hume was not dropped, but he got his way with Smith (and Carlyle would be given a prominent place in the murals in the interior). So, as the exterior strained to be some kind of historical narrative, Edinburgh got its statues of Hume (by James Pittendrigh Macgillivray, and Smith by Henry Snell Gamley, who reworked it from a piece begun by Charles McBride who had died before he completed it.

Of the eight sculptors involved in this work, only Pittendrigh Macgillivray would now be perceived as a substantial figure in the history of European sculpture, someone who might be mentioned in the same breath as Rodin. Although he appears to have liked red sandstone, which he used for the arched gateway to his home, Ravelston Elms, in the west of Edinburgh, its insistent colour makes his work on the Portrait Gallery difficult to place in the wider context of Renaissance and post-Renaissance sculpture. It may be that the demand for historical accuracy in the costume of his figures inhibited his instincts towards more expressive forms.

It is possible, however, to sense some echoes of the great sculpture of the

50 William Hole
at work on the
processional frieze
in 1898

past – for instance, Birnie Rhind cleverly fits his three figures of Mary, Queen of Scots and her courtiers into their narrow niche, while making use of the space outside the niche, with some of the ease that characterises Verrocchio's Christ and St Thomas on the façade of Or San Michele in Florence; again, where John Hutchison is enticed by the abstract qualities of John Knox's gown, both this area and the thrust of the feet and hands carry a suggestion of Donatello's Jeremiah on the same building [49]. But generally, it is sculpture at the end of a tradition, with little hint of the modern forces that were struggling to birth on, say, the British Medical Association building in London where Jacob Epstein began carving the allegorical full-length figures in 1907 that would create such a scandal just a couple of years after the last Portrait Gallery statue was put in place.

PAINTING AND STAINED GLASS

Whatever gaps and odd combinations marked the sculptural programme on the exterior, the processional frieze that William Brassey Hole would paint in the interior above the main arches of the Great Hall is chronological and comprehensive to an extraordinary degree [50]. Completed within a year of Hole receiving the commission in April 1897 to carry out a vast scheme of mural decoration in both the Great Hall and ambulatory, the procession of 155 full-length figures marches in reverse time, clockwise, from Thomas Carlyle to a Stone Age axeman, whose hound prowls in the trees behind him, the only hint of a setting for the long line of Scottish heroes [51]. They tread a grassy field before a shining golden sky, where their names are clearly inscribed (unlike the statues on the exterior). The central focus is a seated female, Caledonia, to whom the Stone Age folk turn with a suggestion of veneration; if she stood she would be a giantess by comparison. Her corselet and head dress are also gilded and she pulls aside a curtain to reveal a

PIVS LOLLIVS ... TACITVS ... BRONZE AGE STONE AGE ... CALEDON

ABERCROMBIE MOORE JEFFREY SCOTT BURNS TELFORD BRUCE DUNCAN CULLEN SMITH FORBES Geo MURRAY CLUNY FLOR MACDON
RK LYNEDOCH RAEBURN HUNTER HUTTON WATT ADAM BOSWELL ROBERTSON HUME

JAMES VI BUCHANAN MURRAY MORTON LETHINGTON MARY MARY OF GUISE JAMES V JAMES IV DUNBAR BLIND ARCHD COCHRAN JAM
DRUMOND NAPIER KNOX RIZZIO BOTHWELL DARNLEY BEATON GAV DOUGLAS MARGARET HARRY BELL THE CAT ALBANY

EDWARD LIDDESDALE RANDOLPH JAMES ROBT BRUCE WALLACE JOHN EDWARD I BRUCE THOMAS ALEXANDER III WILLIAM DAVID I MARG
BALLIOL MORAY OF DAVID II MORAY DOUG-LAS C'TESS BUCHAN BALLIOL OF ANNAN-DALE MAID OF NOR-WAY THE RHYMER ALEXR II THE LION ALEXAN MAL
BOTH-WELL MALCOLM DER I
THE MAIDEN

SIMPSON BREWSTER DALHOL HAMIL CHALMERS WILKIE STEVENSON CAMPBELL
SIE TON

RAMSAY MAR ARGYLL DUNDEE LAUDER CHARLES II MONTROSE LESLIE CHARLES I
THOMSON FLETCHER STAIR JAMES VII DALE LEIGHTON ARGYLL JAMESONE LOTHIAN

BOYD MARIE JAMES II JAMES I DONALD OF ROTHESAY ALBANY DOUGLAS ROBERT
CREIGHTON LIVINGSTON JOANNA THE ISLES ROBERT III BARBOUR II

DUNCAN VIKINGS KENNETH CUTHBERT COLUMBA BRUDE REDEREOH NINIAN
JACH ADAMNAN AIDAN KENTIGERN DRUID THEODOSIUS

51 The processional frieze
by William Hole, 1898

star-sprinkled sky, something that would be taken up in the coffered ceiling of the hall. Her sword is set aside, and she holds a great book against her thighs, the story, presumably, of the future – the past that would be the Portrait Gallery's main concern.

The golden background to the figures in the painted frieze, not flat but insistently rippled, is perhaps a nod towards the schemes of mosaic decoration that both Lord Bute and Lord Lothian had initially promoted. When Findlay had offered the Board of Manufactures a further £10,000 in December 1895 for the embellishment of the exterior and interior of the building, he had suggested that murals might be placed in the Great Hall, ambulatory and ceiling. This early notion is more or less what prevailed, but in the meantime more extravagant ideas were aired. In response to a report prepared by Rowand Anderson for the Portrait Gallery committee in the spring of 1896, Lothian stated a preference for 'real mosaic work'. This was also a preference held by Arthur Halkett, another member of the committee. Lothian went on to make a number of suggestions that sound completely contradictory. The first two were for allegorical subjects, or 'decoration like that of Raphael in the Vatican', which sounds as if he had in mind the ceilings of the Stanze della Segnatura, which are actually a mixture of mosaic and painting. He then proposed, with no show of consistency, something like 'the splendid masterpieces in the East where no figures are used at all'; this would give 'infinite scope for the effective use of colour'. He then remarked, mistakenly, 'that painting would not last long in our climate – it would become dim and heavy …' It is possible that he had true fresco in mind, where the paint combines with a layer of wet plaster. This

52 Removal of a section of *The Battle of Largs* to create a doorway

had proved a disaster in the Palace of Westminster in the 1850s; but the murals on a hard gesso base eventually painted by William Hole proved remarkably durable, later requiring minimal cleaning – and the only 'damage' quite deliberate, though regrettable. This happened when a decision was taken in 1984 to break down the second of those barriers between the two halves of the building that Findlay had insisted on, and insert a narrow doorway in the middle of the east wall of the ambulatory in order to make the lift accessible at first-floor level [52]. This meant the clinical removal of most of the stone-throwing Scot in the centre of the depiction of *The Battle of Largs* (the fragment has been carefully preserved).

In his report to the committee, Rowand Anderson had suggested experimenting with gesso work 'on a small portion of brickwork of the interior walls'. This was presumably done, and this was how the work proceeded. Rowand Anderson had, in fact, been wholeheartedly supported in this by Robert Murdoch Smith, the same man who had tried to exclude the statue of Hume. The architect also proposed two

53 *The Good Deeds of King David I* by William Hole, 1901

54 *The Mission of St Columba* by William Hole, 1901

possible artists and compiled a list of 117 subjects for the frieze. Commemorating them in this way, he stated, would not involve the expense of a statue. The artists in question were Robert Burns and William Burn Murdoch but neither was chosen, apparently deemed too 'celtic' in their inspiration. It is worth remarking here that when the possibility of including mural paintings was first discussed, the architectural historian and Professor of Fine Art at the University of Edinburgh, Gerald Baldwin Brown, had suggested to the Edinburgh Social Union that the Scottish woman artist, Phoebe Anna Traquair should decorate the Great Hall of the Portrait Gallery. She was at the time about to begin work on her masterpiece, the murals of religious subjects that were to fill the walls of the nearby Catholic Apostolic Church (another of Rowand Anderson's buildings). If she had agreed she might well have been chosen but, in the event, she declared that 'desirable as the work was, it was not for her to do it'. When the Board finally made a decision they chose William Hole, who was essentially an illustrator rather than an imaginative artist of Traquair's calibre.

The frieze complete, Hole started the history paintings that fill the walls of the first floor ambulatory. The Board had approved Hole's list of seventeen subjects in February 1898, but in 1900 a decision was made to confine the cycle to the ambulatory, so that only seven were carried out. Along with eight subjects dropped at an early stage, the entire series would have illustrated a story stretching from St Columba to Prince Charles Edward Stuart. The ones that were completed have a bias towards the warlike. From the north-east corner reading in a clockwise direction the subjects were: *The Mission of St Columba* [54]; *The Landing of Queen Margaret at Queensferry*; *The Battle of Largs*; *The Good Deeds of King David I* [53]; *The Battle of Stirling Bridge*; *The Battle of Bannockburn*; and *The Marriage of James IV*. Two narrow upright panels on the north wall, *The Ballad* and *The Pibroch*, seem to have been an afterthought and are something of an oddity in the narrative. Hole's approach to these episodes in Scottish history was so carefully antiquarian that the quantity of information – on arms and costumes, for example – took them outside the realm of true history painting. The battle scenes in particular are wonderfully intricate but lack fire; there is little that engages emotionally. They are subdued in colour and flat in tone, a quite deliberate strategy to ape the effect of tapestry, something that is emphasised by the wide floral and leafy borders that frame them. Hole had visited Europe in 1897 prior to beginning the work, to look at genuine fresco painting in Italy and modern, mural painting in France, particularly Paris where he would have examined Puvis de Chavanne's work in the Panthéon, the church reconstructed as a pantheon for the great men of France in 1791. Puvis, whose work was also well known to the Glasgow Boys, is the continental artist to whom Hole is closest.

Hole's murals were painted either directly onto prepared plaster or onto canvas stuck to the plaster. They were first noticed shortly after completion by W. Matthews Gilbert in an article for the *Art Journal* of 1902/3. Gilbert gives a clear description of the technical processes involved, which he had been given by Hole: 'The walls are grounded with wax; a substance which, with oil of spikenard, is also used in the grinding of colours, with the result that the surfaces are "matt", and not shining as in work in oils. This, however, fits in well with the general decorative plan, which is meant to be flat in effect, like a piece of tapestry with an even distribution of light and shade.' At about the same time James Caw, who had succeeded John Miller Gray as Curator in 1895, produced a little booklet of twenty-four pages (price six pence) on the murals, where his verdict is that they are 'a happy compromise between the rival claims of decoration and representation' – a subtle verdict that reinforces the belief that 'meaning' was the crucial element in the schemes of embellishment which had been carried out on the building, and that 'decoration' was in itself an inadequate term. Sadly, John Ritchie Findlay had died on 16 October 1898 as this work was progressing, work which would bring to fruition all the seeds he had planted. However, Gilbert in the *Art Journal* was able to note that Findlay 'had … seen and warmly commended the frieze and one of the frescoes …'

The painting of the interior was completed by work in the spandrels between the adjacent arches at both ground and first-floor level, and in the coffers of the ceiling. In the spandrels beneath the frieze Hole painted the arms of the twelve royal burghs, derived from the illustrations in *Arms of the Royal and Parliamentary Burghs of Scotland* (published in 1897), by Lord Bute and others. In the equivalent spandrels in the floor above were painted the arms of twelve queens of Scotland, ranging from Elizabeth Muir, queen of Robert II to Mary of Modena, queen of James VII, while on the reverse side of these spandrels, visible only from within the walkway, were positioned the arms of eight members of the Scottish nobility of the fourteenth and fifteenth centuries. In addition, on the south wall above the windows at this level and also in the spandrels on both sides of the arcade on the north side of the ambulatory, and on the north wall itself, are the arms of ten other members of the nobility, again all from the medieval period.

Findlay had been lukewarm over the inclusion of heraldic representations and referred the matter to Lord Bute, who, of course, was exceptionally keen. So also was Lord Lothian. Crucially, however, Rowand Anderson vigorously pursued the idea for the exterior, and a variety of coats of arms for Scottish towns and Scottish institutions (for example, the Royal College of Surgeons of Edinburgh) were carved on the buttress angles of all four towers. The majority of the corbels beneath each statue were also given arms (or mottoes), often within complex leafy and figural settings. Finally, the arms of the Society of Antiquaries of Scotland were inserted above the ground-floor doorway in the east wall of the Great Hall, at that time the only entrance to the Museum of Antiquities that Findlay had allowed.

There had also been a certain amount of discussion about the use of stained glass throughout the building. Findlay himself had preferred that windows should remain plain, so as to maximise the light – and a feeling had persisted that the hall was too dark. A decision seems to have been made, however, that the inclusion of any stained glass should be delayed until all of the other embellishments had been carried out. In the event, three small armorial glass panels designed by William Graham Boss, which had been gifted by the committee of the Heraldic Exhibition

held in the Portrait Gallery in 1893, were inserted in the small quatrefoil windows above the main windows on the south side of the ambulatory. Two others were bequeathed by John Miller Gray who had died in 1894.

Two final elements were added to the artwork the building had become, one in glass and one painted. Having been long reconciled to the presence of the Museum of Antiquities in his Portrait Gallery, Findlay commissioned a memorial window to mark the opening of the Museum on 13 August 1891 [140]. But, with a nice irony (and was the irony perhaps Findlay's?), it consisted of twenty-three portraits of office bearers of the Society of Antiquaries of Scotland plus their patron, Queen Victoria. Inserted in 1894 in the large window on the penultimate landing of the eastern staircase, the portraits were also the work of the glass painter, William Graham Boss. Entirely graphic in style, the 'medallions' are set amidst flowers and plants. Among the subjects were many of the principal players in the game of founding a portrait gallery: Findlay himself, Rowand Anderson, Noël Paton, Fettes Douglas and Lords Lothian and Bute [9–14]. It is a line-up that illuminates the interconnectedness of the cultural and artistic milieu of Scotland at this time.

Finally, following a proposal made in 1897, William Hole opened up the coffers of the ceiling in the Great Hall to 'the northern sidereal hemisphere' [55]. As he described it, 'the astronomical figures of the constellations and the intervening spaces are rendered in varying tints of blue with embossed gold stars [they are in fact attached mouldings rather than embossed], the roof beams being coloured golden brown with slight touches of gilding …' There is a parallel here, of course, to the more spectacular celestial ceiling at Rowand Anderson's Mount Stuart, where the stars are actually piercings in the ceilings, lit from behind. In terms of message, the more sober Findlay had insisted that the signs of the zodiac should be kept subdued.

Much later, when most of those who had wrestled with the completion of this intricate icon of national sentiment had departed the scene, three further armorial sections of glass were placed in the window of the central hall. Designed by Margaret Chilton, aided by the glass painter Douglas Strachan from Aberdeen, these represented the arms of Mary, Queen of Scots (once more), the Scottish variant of the royal arms of Great Britain, and the pre-Union royal arms of Scotland – themes that had much earlier been carved into the main portal. The inclusion of these windows marked the reopening of the Portrait Gallery in July 1934 after the three years of closure for fireproofing.

The relative darkness of the Great Hall had always been a problem, especially when viewing the processional frieze. The visibility of this frieze was much enhanced by modern spot-lighting in the early 1980s, although the system was difficult to maintain and also obtrusive in relation to the internal architecture of this great space. At about the same time the ambient light was improved by hanging four large lanterns from the central beams of the coffered ceiling. These lanterns were replicated from a lamp made for the Church of St John the Evangelist at the west end of Edinburgh in 1935 to a design by the painter, and trustee, D.Y. Cameron.

55 The ceiling of the Great Hall

CHAPTER FOUR

THE LATER USE OF
THE BUILDING

ROWAND Anderson's red sandstone building is a striking landmark at the east end of Queen Street, its Gothic Revival elaboration in marked contrast to the Georgian simplicity of the mingled terraced houses and flats that make up the rest of the half-mile-long street. It is a contrast which its planners must always have been conscious of, but there is little evidence that any profound thought was given to how suitable the interior would be for the display of a collection of paintings, small at the time, which was bound to grow considerably. The National Gallery on the Mound must have provided clear enough evidence of the need for uninterrupted wall space to display paintings, yet the ground floor and first floor of the new building were profusely glazed both front and rear. At ground-floor level each wall on either side of the main entrance hall was pierced by four large, arched windows. This arrangement was repeated at the back of the building, but with one window less in each section. Surmounting this at first-floor level was an arcade of virtually continuous glazing, broken only by niches for statues and slim pilasters [56]. This system of fenestration, with some simplification, was continued at both gable ends and at the rear, wrapping the entire building in almost continuous glass at this level – a surprisingly modern feature if the Gothic details are ignored.

The number of almost continuous window openings at these two levels meant a severe shortage of hanging surfaces in the interior. This was compounded by the central interior walls at both levels also being pierced by grand arches, with only a few feet of available wall space between them. As the collection began to grow, which it did quite quickly, the problem soon became apparent – and it has continued throughout the Portrait Gallery's life.

The few early illustrations of the interior show that almost immediately moveable wooden screens were inserted which projected into the galleries from the narrow spaces between the windows [57, 58]. These screens were evidently large enough to allow an arrangement of two tiers of three head and shoulders portraits packed frame to frame, though not quite to the floor (in the 1890s such congestion remained acceptable). Although no plans for these screens survive, they must have measured in the region of 9 feet square. Where smaller items were hung, a little space between pictures was possible, though there was evidently no worry about having the lower edges close to the floor. The unbroken end walls, of course, were not a problem, and here far more pictures could be hung – typically, three-quarter length portraits hung near floor level with full-lengths squeezed above – reaching a total height from floor level of about 16 feet. This arrangement had the effect of placing the bottom of full-length portraits substantially above average eye-level, thus placing any consideration of the quality of a portrait well out of reach. This is

56 The Portrait Gallery showing the extent of the windows.

unlikely to have caused much concern, however, since in the 'pre-modern' climate of the time a distinction between the representation of the subject (that is, the portrayal or narrative aspect of the painting) and any kind of independent aesthetic value that the portrait might have is unlikely to have loomed very large. This distinction, which is now commonplace, relates of course to the truism (discussed below) that the quality of a painting is of little moment if there is good reason to think a likeness has been established– a continuation of Carlyle's belief that virtually any image would do provided it was made from life.

In the course of the twentieth century two principal attempts were made to solve the problem of insufficient hanging space in the ground-and first-floor rooms. The first was made in the early 1930s by Stanley Cursiter, at that time the curator in charge of the Portrait Gallery. Cursiter was a painter of considerable accomplishment, and also a man of inventive and practical ingenuity. His solution was to erect a series of brick and plaster, wedge-shaped screens that jutted into both rooms from the narrow wall spaces between the windows and from the walls of the central arcades [59]. The arrangement created a series of open hexagons. Each hanging surface was carefully angled towards the daylight, while artificial light was provided by a bank of lamps hidden in the tops of the screens, directed towards the ceiling from where it was reflected throughout the room. It was ingenious, but the screens were inadequate in size – they could scarcely accommodate a full-length portrait, and made any kind of narrative grouping of the portraits difficult. This

THE SCOTSMAN, SATURDAY, APRIL 9, 1949.

REOPENING OF NATIONAL PORTRAIT GALLERY

Part of the ground floor gallery of the Scottish National Portrait Gallery in Queen Street, Edinburgh, which was reopened to the public yesterday. It is expected that the entire Gallery will be reopened within the next few months.

57 The view of the ground-floor gallery showing the original temporary screens, *c*.1900
© RCAHMS
(Henry Bedford Lemere Collection)

58 The same view showing post 1925 amendments to the temporary screens
SNPG Reference Section

59 The same view showing the wedge-shaped permanent screens erected in the 1930s
National Library of Scotland

60 The final hanging
screens constructed
in the 1980s
© Crown Copyright:
RCAHMS

configuration of these two rooms remained in place until the early 1980s when the
wedge-shaped screens were removed. They were replaced by much taller (some
16 feet) steel-framed and wooden-clad screens, and jutted much further into the
rooms at right angles [60]. In addition, they continued across the window openings. This created a series of rectangular spaces (six on the ground floor and seven
on the first floor) opening into each other down the central axis of the room and
through the central arches. Covered in fabric or painted, these screens, in effect
internal walls, allowed far greater continuity in the placing of the portraits or other
works, which became especially important as the number of thematic loan exhibitions increased. One major drawback of course was the loss of natural light and any
feeling of the world outside. Lighting was now provided by a continuous track, the
fittings carefully angled to wash each wall with evenly distributed light.

These modifications were all predicated on the evolving functions of the Portrait
Gallery – never static in either the size of the collection, approaches to display
and interpretation, or a growing programme of temporary loan exhibitions. These
changing demands had to grapple with the constraints imposed by a building
which, though custom built, never took enough account of everyday practicali-
ties. It may be that the problem was not foreseen because public portrait galleries
with narrative, didactic aims were a relatively new invention, with little in the way
of precedent on how their function should be accommodated. The kind of re-
invention that was attempted during the twentieth century has continued. In 2009
when the building was closed for the massive re-configuration and conservation
project which was given the title 'Portrait of a Nation', a group of young graffiti
artists was turned loose in the ground-floor gallery to create, with a noisy fanfare
of destruction, fantasies with social and historical undertones on every surface.

Some cut windows into strange worlds in walls that had recently held the familiar icons of Scotland's history, and every surface was covered with a temporary beauty before the builders moved in to gut the principal galleries and install the latest solution [61].

The problems and re-configurations described above did not, of course, apply to anything like the same extent to the second (or top) floor of the building when it came into use as the collection expanded. This was the 'classical' slice of the neo-Gothic building, with unbroken wall areas throughout the three rooms: the central gallery (usually referred to as the Square Room or, later, the Raeburn Room) which sat above the Great Hall and extended to the north front through an open arcade; and the longitudinal galleries to the north and south of the central spine which opened into the small rooms in the western transverse wing that ultimately became curatorial offices. All three rooms were top-lit, the Square Room by a square, pyramidal cupola, the other two galleries by high, coved lights running the whole length of each room [62, 64].

Although well lit and providing plenty of hanging space, these galleries were not entirely without their problems, and as modern museological methods came into play and pressures on space increased, various adaptations were made. The original plain tongue-and-groove shuttering on the walls of the Square Room soon came to be regarded as unsightly and was covered with canvas and painted, and a knee-high dado was installed that continued round the other galleries. A more fundamental change took place in the immediate post-war period when the arcade on the north side of the Square Room was filled in to create a picture store, something to which little thought had been given in the original design of the building. At the same time a bank of radiators was placed in the centre of this gallery, surrounded by

61 The destruction of the hanging screens during the *Rough Cut Nation* project in 2009

62 The Square Room showing Robert Rowand Anderson's original arcade, *c.*1900
© RCAHMS (Henry Bedford Lemere Collection

63 Coved light in room four
SNPG Reference Section

64 The Square Room
with the arcade
blocked off

© Crown Copyright:
RCAHMS

65 Stanley Cursiter's
lay-lights in room four

SNPG Reference Section

seating. In more recent times, when concerts and events that required staging and seating became common, this feature became a real impediment and was removed. At the same time the Square Room was air-conditioned – the only room in the entire building to be so treated before the twenty-first century.

As the dangers of ultra-violet light to paintings came to be more appreciated, a need to control the significant quantities of sunlight entering through the large skylights became more and more apparent [63]. In the Square Room this was tackled by simply whitewashing the glazing at the beginning of the summer and removing it as winter approached! In the renovations of the 1980s this laborious method was ended, and the newly glazed cupola was coated with translucent film. The solution to the problem in the two longitudinal galleries was once again devised by the ever-inventive Stanley Cursiter. It was ingenious for its time and also radically altered the appearance of the two rooms, giving them a much more modern feel. Based on what he had seen installed in the Museum Boijmans van Beuningen in Rotterdam, he suspended a flat ceiling beneath the original coved ceilings which, as a result, disappeared from view. The light from the roof now travelled to the walls through a series of tight-packed louvres (slatted apertures) which were carefully angled so that no direct sunlight reached the paintings. In the centre of this ceiling was a series of flat lay-lights of translucent glass, running virtually the entire length of each room, above which were arranged groups of fluorescent tubes which provided a boost to the daylight when required [65]. The forms of this ceiling were essentially art deco, a theme which was continued when, again in the 1980s, the old-fashioned hanging rails were removed and the walls panelled and lined in fabric.

The lack of adequate storage space has already been touched on. The basement, so beloved of journalists who imagine it filled with hidden treasures, did not physically exist on the Portrait Gallery side of the building, although there was one in the Museum of Antiquities. In the reconfiguration of the 1930s a properly equipped store had been created in the section of the ground-floor gallery nearest the main entrance. The storage area inserted behind the blocked-up arcade of the Square Room on the top floor in the immediate post-war period held a great many paintings, but the storage system was poor and it was not until the 1980s that proper sliding screens were installed. At the same time another modern store was created at the west end of the building, in a room formerly used by the Board of Trustees, who had quit their small corner of the Portrait Gallery in 1972. The lack of storage space was further eased when the Museum of Antiquities began their long, slow withdrawal from the building after their rebirth (in a dedicated building) as the Museum of Scotland, amalgamated with the Royal Museum of Scotland in Chambers Street. The Museum had ceded a small area of the ground floor (subsequently extended) so that in 1990 the Portrait Gallery could create a restaurant – the enormously successful Queen Street Café, which was celebrated in a joyful painting by John Bellany. In the late 1990s the Museum relinquished the remainder of their ground-floor gallery, which provided a good deal of extra display space for temporary installations and exhibitions – the first time in virtually a century that loan exhibitions (though only small ones) could be mounted without dismantling parts of the permanent collection. This move also allowed the construction of another storage area.

Much of what has been described is a story of modification and adaptation, perhaps to a greater degree than was usual in nineteenth-century creations, all of which have had to cope with growing collections and the challenges of modernity. Museums and picture galleries (and the Portrait Gallery was a mixture of these) are living organisms whose deepest concerns are with time and change, but they also require a stability which enables them to cope with the requirements of their society. There is, it has to be admitted, a certain irony in the fact that the Scottish National Portrait Gallery had to undergo so much change in even its earliest days despite being housed in a dedicated building, a fact that enabled it to claim the honour of having been the first purpose-built national portrait gallery in the world. (The National Portrait Gallery in London did not move into its permanent premises until 1896.) The piecemeal and patchwork impression that is gained in taking this long backwards look over more than a dozen decades is also in part a reflection of the fact that there was always a cuckoo in the nest – the Society of Antiquaries and the Museum founded on their collections, the Museum of Antiquities. Findlay, though himself a member of the Society, had always insisted that the Gallery and the Museum be kept distinct, with as many impediments as possible to any obvious linking of the two, notably the absence of any doorway between them at first-floor or top-floor level. Curiously (but it may be no coincidence), the benefactor who paid for the Portrait Gallery in London, W.H. Alexander, also insisted that there should be 'no communication whatever with the National Gallery', round which his building was wrapped. In the public's perception, however, the Portrait Gallery in Edinburgh and the Museum of Antiquities did in fact tend to merge, so that the building came to be perceived by many as simply 'the Museum' or the 'Queen Street Museum'. Indeed, as justification for the change of direction that had been forced on Findlay, the powers of the time began to stress that the collections of portraits and antiquities were natural bedfellows and would benefit from being seen together. This was a view that was never far from the surface until the physical separation that followed the creation of the Museum of Scotland in 1998. Of course, as each institution was concerned with Scottish history there was much in common between them, but they remained pretty much apart, with only intermittent collaboration. This usually took the form of shared exhibitions, the most spectacular of which was *Dynasty* in 1990, when portraits and artefacts were totally integrated to tell the story of the Stuarts. This was an effort actively supported by the civil servants in Scottish Office who at that time harboured vague thoughts of uniting the two institutions. Whatever their thinking, when this final shared endeavour came to be dismantled, many wondered if an opportunity was being lost for ever. Yet, whatever ambiguities in identity there may have been, perhaps compounded by the Portrait Gallery's management being part of a larger entity, the National Galleries of Scotland, it grew enormously in public affection throughout the twentieth century. When, in the first decade of the twenty-first century, the entire building that Findlay had attempted to dedicate solely to a National Portrait Gallery became at last fully available, the opportunity arose to both fulfil Findlay's vision and to develop it in entirely new directions.

THE BUILDING MADE WHOLE

The undertaking by government to fund the redevelopment of Findlay's building came in 2006, and plans were drawn up by the Glasgow-based firm of architects, Page\Park that would cost £17.6 million. This sum was made up by an initial contribution of £5.1 million from the Scottish Government (increased by a further £2 million in 2011), £4.8 million from the Heritage Lottery Fund, and the remainder from trusts, corporate sources and individuals. William Hole's frieze was imaginatively put to use in fund-raising by 'selling' the historical figures for specified sums to donors, so that their affection for the Portrait Gallery and their favourite Scot would be expressed in a visible form. Donors could also acquire a stake in individual stars on the celestial ceiling.

In essence, the scheme was the unification of the two parts of a single building that in architectural terms had been kept uncomfortably separate; and sentimentalists might see it as a kind of 'homecoming' for the Portrait Gallery. It certainly represented a degree of commitment by the Scottish Government that in the Gallery's recent history had not always been whole-hearted. The Gallery now entered another period of enforced closure, but this time for entirely positive reasons. It closed its doors in the quite spectacular way described above in April 2009 and re-opened to visitors in December 2011.

Inevitably, the work involved much opening-up, some of it restoration in the conventional sense, some of it spectacularly innovative [66–71]. Perhaps the most striking, and certainly the most immediately visible feature, has been the creation of new vistas by piercing both the east and west walls of the vestibule and the two main structural walls that stand a short distance behind. This means that after only a few steps over the threshold the visitor, by looking both left and right, can gain a sense of virtually the entire length of the building. Although the original cramped, rather dark vestibule, leading by three doorways into the Great Hall, was a distinctive feature of Findlay's (and Anderson's) building, this relaxing of the space, which so obviously pulls the building together, is something that could be said to match Findlay's very earliest aspiration for the Portrait Gallery. The great volume of the two high-ceilinged galleries on the ground floor of the building was ingeniously exploited by the insertion of mezzanine floors in the southern half of each of these galleries, creating a visual interplay between voids on the north, or street side, of the building and 'stacked' space at the rear. In this way rooms in the eastern half of the building that introduce the collection and feature contemporary Scottish history, along with a large educational area, sit beneath a mezzanine layer given over to storage and recreational spaces. The section of this reconfigured ground-floor gallery which lies nearest the foot of the staircase has been given over to lavatory accommodation, solving at a stroke the inadequacies that had been cause for constant, sometimes amusing, complaint over many years. This section is

66 The Square Room after refurbishment with the original arcade reinstated

67 The eastern section of one of the first floor galleries

Clockwise from top left:

68 View from the mezzanine looking down to the Contemporary Gallery

69 The new glass lift at first-floor level

70 The Photography Gallery

71 One of the first floor galleries

accessed from the Great Hall through the entrance that Findlay had decreed should be the only link between the Portrait Gallery and the Museum of Antiquities.

The western half of the ground floor (where, as in the eastern half, the wooden parquet floors have been replaced with grey stone slabs) has been largely given over to an extensive shop and café, the latter spreading through a new opening into the transverse area in the south-west corner of the building. Above this, again in the southern half of the Gallery, is the other mezzanine floor. These new mezzanine floors can be read as a quite natural enlargement of the floor area of the interior of the building because of their linkages through new openings with the existing mezzanine levels in the lateral wings of the building. The principal access to these two new floors is by doorways created on the half-landings of either staircase. From these half-landings, access has also been provided to the cluster of existing mezzanine rooms above the main entrance. Here, because of rather odd variations in the old levels, gently sloped ramps now tie these rooms together. These new rooms are 'encased' in glass, with all of the new, visible, supporting steelwork painted in an intense grey, which is complementary in colour to areas of newly exposed brickwork. This same grey now emphasises the steel beams of the early twentieth-century reconstruction that were left visible in the eastern section of the building. This 'old' steel is a reminder that the Portrait Gallery was virtually contemporary with the Eiffel Tower and the Forth Railway Bridge.

The galleries at first-floor level have undergone very little re-configuration – with one notable exception. The elaborately cased library that had once served the Museum of Antiquities has been carefully dismantled and re-installed in the old Portrait Gallery part of the building. Taken down from the top floor, and rebuilt with very little modification to its intricate woodwork, and with its elevated balcony on all four sides retained, it has reappeared here with a sense of always having belonged [132]. Now, of course, necessarily sealed off from the other half of this gallery, it might be recalled that Findlay was quite upset when he saw that the three central arches that make up the spine of this room had been filled in. In fact the three great arches, although closed off, are still clearly present when viewed from the other side, and retain most of their spatial identity. This half of the original gallery has been made into a dedicated photography gallery. Both the repositioned library and the photography area are now linked by two doorways (one of them new) to the original Print Room, which has been completely re-equipped.

The end-to-end opening-up of the building that has created a new sense of spaciousness on the ground floor has been repeated on the top floor. When the building was opened in 1889, the large central room which sits above the ceiling of the Great Hall consisted of a room that was square in plan, but with an extension to the north wall through a lateral arcade that became known as 'the annexe to the square room'. Shortly after the Second World War, when the annexe was sealed off and converted to a picture store, the arcade vanished. In the current renovation this was uncovered, and the two end walls of the annexe were pierced with new doorways, again emphasising the unification of the building. But this sense of

vista was carried even further than on the ground floor with the creation of new openings on the same line, leading into the transverse galleries at either end of the building. With glances to both left and right, the visitor can therefore now encompass the entire seventy-six yards of Rowand Anderson's interior.

The problems over the provision of a lift in a building of three floors have already been noted – at first it was not considered necessary, and then it was far too small when fitted into the 'chase' that Anderson had provided near the eastern staircase. Now, however, immediately behind the staircase, all three floors have been broken open and a glass-encased lift shaft has been constructed, rising from ground-floor level and continuing up in a highly visible fashion to the top floor. The lift itself carries as many as forty-eight passengers – with more than sufficient room for the lift attendant that civil servants had deemed necessary in 1930.

72 The entrance to the Great Hall, and, on the left the Contemporary Gallery

NUNQUAM INUTILIS
EST OPERA CIVIS BONI

IN MEMORY OF JOHN RITCHIE FINDLAY
THE FOUNDER OF THE NATIONAL
PORTRAIT GALLERY OF SCOTLAND
AND DONOR OF THIS BUILDING

CHAPTER FIVE

CONSTITUTION
AND MANAGEMENT

THE constitution and management of the Scottish National Portrait Gallery has always differed in one important respect from its counterpart in London. From its inception it has been either an extension of an existing entity, the Scottish National Gallery, or embedded in a larger entity, the National Galleries of Scotland. This new institution, created by the British Parliament by an Act of 1906 and placed under the control of a Board of Trustees, was constituted by the Secretary for Scotland on 30 March 1907. It grew in complexity throughout the twentieth century, with an expansion of its original functions, the principal ones being the setting up of a Print Room in 1950 and the creation of a Gallery of Modern Art in 1960. These were developments which affected the Portrait Gallery, sometimes imperceptibly and sometimes in quite direct ways. For example, the Print Room was conceived initially as a 'Scottish Print Room' with the intention that it should be located in the Portrait Gallery (and would have been additional to the Portrait Gallery's own Print Room). This did not happen, and in due course it became part of the National Gallery with a dedicated Keeper – encompassing English and European prints and drawings as well as Scottish material. In addition, even from the years before the Second World War, the trustees had aimed at setting up a Gallery of Modern Art. The case for this was pressed tirelessly by Stanley Cursiter, who had already left his mark on the reconfiguration of the interior of the Portrait Gallery. Initially, there was no prospect of funding for this gallery – indeed the Treasury had stated that it would have to rely on private benefaction – but throughout the Second World War the trustees badgered the Ministry of Works to acquire groups of adjacent town houses, and latterly the University Club at 127 Princes Street (another Anderson building), as premises for a modern collection. These premises were intended to be only a temporary measure, however. The ultimate aim was an entirely new building on what was known as the York Buildings site, immediately opposite the Portrait Gallery [34]. Plans had earlier been prepared by the architect Alan Reiach, and even the Ministry of Works had been persuaded to produce plans for this site as late as 1950, during the brief tenure of Ellis Waterhouse as Director of the National Galleries of Scotland. Waterhouse saw this proximity to the Portrait Gallery (where it was still at this time intended to house the Print Room) as a great virtue – but it was not to be, and ten years would pass before a Gallery of Modern Art was opened in a modest house in the Royal Botanic Garden.

This is one of the 'ifs' in the history of the Portrait Gallery. What effect would a Gallery of Modern Art nearby have had on the profile of visitors and the range of activities at the Portrait Gallery, which is sometimes seen as too distant from the centre of things? Would the term 'art centre', once used of the Mound, have come to

73 The Findlay
Memorial

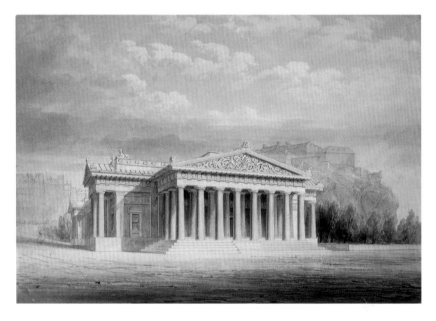

74 *Edinburgh Castle and the Proposed Scottish National Gallery* by William Henry Playfair

Scottish National Gallery
W.F. Watson Bequest in 1886, D 2419

75 *The Royal Institution* by George Meikle Kemp, about 1840

Scottish National Gallery
Bought in 1946, D 4264

76 Early view of the Scottish National Portrait Gallery from the west

© RCAHMS (Francis M. Chrystal Collection)

be applied to the east end of Queen Street? This might seem idle speculation, but all these issues emphasise that the history of the Portrait Gallery is part of the history of the National Galleries of Scotland and of the histories of the other two parts of that body. It is an unusual situation, though the strains have been few. Calls might have been expected to give the Portrait Gallery independence, and the question has arisen on one or two occasions, but it has never become a major issue. The degree of autonomy has varied over the years, but this has mainly been an expression of the personalities involved in the day-to-day curatorial management of the galleries.

When John Miller Gray was appointed Curator of the Portrait Gallery early in 1884, his counterpart at the National Gallery was Gourlay Steell, an animal painter of no great note and the last but one of the five Royal Scottish Academicians to hold that post. Although the Scottish National Gallery and the Scottish National Portrait Gallery (still to be built) were both under the control of the commissioners of the Board of Trustees for Fisheries and Manufactures, they were seen at this time as two distinct entities. However, that changed in 1906 when a National Galleries of Scotland Act led to the demise of the Board of Manufactures and its replacement by a Board of Trustees for the National Galleries of Scotland who would manage both the Portrait Gallery and the National Gallery. At the same time the Royal Scottish Academy was moved into the Royal Institution building. All of these arrangements brought an end to the decades of instability as the various bodies had jockeyed for position [74–6].

The new Board of Trustees, seven in number, under the chairmanship of Thomas Gibson Carmichael, held their first meeting in the Royal Institution on 10 April 1907. Among them was a familiar name, John Ritchie Findlay, son of the original donor and someone who was to play a very active role in the affairs of the National Galleries of Scotland. His father had died nine years previously and was memorialised in a pseudo-Renaissance 'altarpiece' containing a posthumous portrait by Sir George Reid [73]. This was something that flew in the face of the founding philosophy of portrait galleries, that the images should be painted from life – 'which he [the artist] saw with this eyes, and which I can never seen with mine', as Thomas Carlyle had expressed it in his famous letter of 1854. The memorial, which has moved from location to location within the Portrait Gallery throughout its history (a rough inscription on the woodwork at the back, perhaps added by the carpenter who made it, records the surrender of Mafeking in 1900) might also have raised an eyebrow of the modest Findlay. Rowand Anderson had actually asked the Board's permission to tone down the bright gold leaf that embellished the memorial and they agreed to this.

The first Curator of the Portrait Gallery, and the only one to bear that title, John Miller Gray, had died in 1894. Apart from setting the young Gallery on its feet, Miller Gray (rumoured to have been in love with the artist Phoebe Anna Traquair who had turned down the opportunity to paint murals in the Great Hall), is best remembered for his book, *James and William Tassie: A Biographical and Critical Sketch*, which was published in the year of his death and is still the standard work on the subject. Gray's place was taken by James Caw, a versatile individual who

77 James Caw by
Edward Drummond
Young, 1936
Commissioned by
the Scottish National
Portrait Gallery in the
1930s
SNPG Reference Section

78 Hew Dalrymple by
Edward Drummond
Young, 1936
Commissioned by
the Scottish National
Portrait Gallery in the
1930s
SNPG Reference Section

would become Director of the National Galleries on the setting up of the new Board in 1907 [77]. In the latter role he was to be paid the not inconsiderable sum of £500 per year. The minutes of that first historic meeting also suggest the swing of the pendulum away from a relatively independent Portrait Gallery to something more embedded in the bigger institution by spelling out Caw's new responsibilities: 'It will be noted that Mr Caw's duties will extend over the National Portrait Gallery, as well as over the National Gallery.'

Despite Caw's versatility, the need for a curator dedicated to the Portrait Gallery was evident, and the following year Thomas Corsan Morton was appointed Assistant Keeper, at £150 a year. Curiously, the Secretary for Scotland overrode the trustees and insisted that the job title should be 'Keeper'. Is there perhaps a hint in the Secretary for Scotland's intervention of a concern for the status of the fledgling Portrait Gallery? It certainly illustrates a close relationship between government and the trustees which was to continue for most of the century, when, especially in the earlier years, permission had to be sought for quite modest expenditure. This was despite the fact that the chairman of the trustees had been made the accounting officer, something that was to continue until 1955 when the Treasury insisted that that responsibility should be taken on by the Director, at that time David Baxandall, who demurred at the idea, on the grounds of his current responsibilities for 'the direction of three institutions housed in three separate buildings'.

Thomas Corsan Morton, the new Keeper, was a minor painter loosely associated with the group of artists known as the Glasgow Boys. A somewhat nebulous figure, he retired in 1925 when he briefly became Director of the Kirkcaldy Art Gallery. There is little evidence of how he interacted with Caw, but it is difficult not to believe that Caw was the dominant partner. Corsan Morton is hardly ever mentioned in the records of board meetings, instructions from the trustees always being addressed to the Director (at this time curators did not attend in person). Whatever their relationship, both Caw and Morton (unlike Miller Gray) were practising artists, continuing the tradition of those members of the Royal Scottish Academy who had run the National Gallery since 1858. That tradition continued when Stanley Cursiter, a painter of considerable distinction, was appointed as successor to Corsan Morton, and, ultimately, Caw, but with the burgeoning of art history as a calling, even a fashionable one, practitioners have become a rarity among gallery curators.

Caw had a scientific bent and trained as an engineering draughtsman. But he was also profoundly attracted to art and took night classes in both Glasgow and Edinburgh; he would go on to exhibit watercolour landscapes at the Royal Scottish Academy over many years. He also had a number of friends among the Glasgow Boys, the closest and most influential being James Guthrie, one of the inaugural trustees of the National Galleries. Not long after his promotion to Director, Caw published a wide-ranging history of Scottish art, *Scottish Painting 1620–1908*, superseded in many ways but still an interesting book. That he was deeply lodged in the Edinburgh art world in a way that is now difficult to imagine is suggested not only by his friendship with Guthrie, but also by his role as art critic of *The Scotsman* (which was still owned by John Ritchie Findlay) from 1916 to 1933, and his marriage in 1909 to Annie McTaggart, the daughter of the Scottish 'impressionist' William McTaggart. It was no doubt because of his 'establishment' in this way that he was able to persuade his trustees to buy for the National Gallery such an extraordinarily modern painting as Gauguin's *The Vision of the Sermon* in 1925.

The principal impression of the Board in the inter-war years and the late 1940s is one of longevity, for the membership changed rarely, and at the end of each five-year cycle they tended to be re-appointed en masse. When they did change it was usually as a result of death or some major alteration in their contribution to society at large: for example, the first chairman, Thomas Gibson Carmichael, had resigned after little more than a year in that position 'on his appointment as Governor of Victoria'; Lord Cooper, who had had his third renewal in 1952, died in post in 1955; and Hew Dalrymple, whose involvement with the Galleries stretched over a period of forty-three years, resigned as chairman early in 1945, shortly before his death later that same year [78]. A couple of months later, the distinguished artist D.Y. Cameron also died after twenty-five years as a trustee. Their fellow members eulogised them both as 'very gentle sincere men', remarking specifically on Dalrymple's 'knowledge of Scottish portraiture'.

The other striking aspect of the Board's activities in these years is the mundane nature of some of the things they involved themselves in, such as appointments of attendant staff (even a housekeeper), the price of postcards, or even the procurement of material for the attendants' uniforms, which was delegated to the only female trustee of these years, Lady Watson. At a slightly more elevated level two trustees – often Dalrymple and Findlay – would prepare the financial estimates for the following year. All of these activities would in the post-war period become the responsibility of the professional staff, which grew vastly in numbers, especially from the 1970s onwards.

The nature of the relationship between the staff and the Board in the inter-war and Second World War period is difficult to gauge. There were more trustees than curators and this must have coloured how things were done. It is difficult now to imagine, for example, a portrait being accepted with the proviso that it might have to be cut down in size at a later date (the portrait of Arthur Mitchell by George Reid). The donor was none too keen on the idea, but left it to the wisdom of the trustees. Such a fate had already befallen another Reid portrait, that of the agriculturalist George Hope which had been cut down on acquisition in 1925. This 'wisdom' had led to a curious, indeed lamentable, course of action in 1924 when a decision was taken to commission copies of important national portraits that were deemed unlikely to ever become available for the collection. A sum of up to £300 was made available for the project. With no hint of a blush it was also specified that the copies should be head and shoulders only, whatever the format of the original portrait. There seems to be no record of how either Caw or Corsan Morton viewed these matters, nor is there any sense of a debate on the question of what constitutes authenticity in our understanding of the past, unless it was suppressed.

This was a debate that did rage briefly under a later directorship, that of Colin Thompson in the late 1970s and early 1980s, when he created two exhibitions at the National Gallery, *Seeing is Believing* and *Lookalike*, on how we react to paintings as residues of the past. A similar type of exhibition, *Eye to Eye*, which dealt exclusively with portrait imagery, was held at the Portrait Gallery in 1979/80. The paintings in all three exhibitions were removed from their usual context and juxtaposed in unexpected ways. Flouting traditional chronologies, the intention was to pose questions about how works of art – even copies and fakes – can be interpreted, and to suggest that there are few limits to how they can be understood. One particular issue raised was the question of authenticity, something that has to inform how any historical museum grapples with the mystery of the past. No matter how convincing a replica, or a copy, its aura is bound to be affected in a negative way by what we know about it.

A much more fruitful initiative was taken at the beginning of 1939 with the creation of an advisory committee, to be concerned exclusively with the affairs of the Portrait Gallery. By this time Stanley Cursiter had been succeeded as Keeper of the Portrait Gallery by Archibald Haswell Miller. Miller had trained at Glasgow School of Art and travelled widely on the Continent before the First World War, when he became an expert on military uniforms. He painted military portraits and landscapes and was an accomplished illustrator. A number of his drawings of portraits in private collections are still in the Gallery's archive. The advice of the new committee, of course, was to be offered to the trustees, who retained the final say on all matters it had dealt with. The committee was no ad hoc affair, its membership appointed by warrant of the Secretary of State for Scotland, who specified that it should consist of two of the existing trustees and 'four persons with qualifications in Scottish history or portraiture'. Its initial membership consisted of Hew Dalrymple (as chairman) and a judge, Stair Gillon, as the trustee members, with Professor Robert Hannay, Kenneth Sanderson (another lawyer), the historian William Douglas Simpson and Major Lord James Thomas Stewart-Murray making up the remainder. However, with war looming it was hardly an auspicious time, and by October of the same year the committee was suspended – and the gallery closed. Nevertheless it continued in an informal way, with Kenneth Sanderson and the trustee D.Y. Cameron keeping an eye on the Portrait Gallery's interests. This attempt at continuity was repeated when Professor Hannay died in 1940, his place being offered to Dr W.H. Meikle, a future Historiographer Royal. As an end to the European war began to seem likely, and with a prospect of the building being re-opened (a false dawn), the committee was re-constituted in March 1945, a number of months before the Second World War actually ended. Its membership remained much as it had been before, the seemingly immortal Hew Dalrymple still in the chair, but with the addition of Victor Hope, 2nd Marquess of Linlithgow.

One of the most intriguing manifestations of the advisory committee's activities at that time was an intervention by William Douglas Simpson early in 1946, when strenuous efforts were still being made to re-open the gallery. It marks one of the occasional swings of the pendulum towards a more autonomous Portrait Gallery. It was Simpson's contention that the gallery's prestige required to be enhanced and the status of its staff improved. Curiously, at the same time moves were underway to create a post of Keeper dedicated solely to the National Gallery, and this prompted Haswell Miller to write to the Board that if this happened he would be left merely as the Keeper of the Portrait Gallery, with 'resultant disadvantages and hardships' that he did not spell out. The Board responded to this by saying that the opposite was the case, for, by 'giving a more independent standing to the Scottish National Portrait Gallery and the efforts at present under consideration for raising its status', his own status would be raised, not diminished. There is a hint here of some kind of collusion between Haswell Miller and Simpson, but that can only be speculation. Dr Simpson's memorandum of June 1946, despatched from King's College, Aberdeen, was considered at the advisory committee on 4 October. His main contention was that 'our Portrait Gallery is graded as a mere branch of the National Picture Gallery', and that it should be 'raised to the ranks of an autonomous institution' with 'the status of its Keeper [raised] to that of a Director'. The committee approved the notion of the Keeper having the status of Director but there is no record of their discussion of the Gallery's autonomy. When the Board discussed the matter three weeks later they shot down the idea of a Director, and appear to have said nothing about autonomy – and it has never been raised in any official channel since. They had, however, at their previous meeting, accepted the

Committee's suggestion of creating an Assistant Keeper post, something which happened in 1951, when Basil Skinner was appointed – thereby doubling the Gallery's curatorial team at a stroke. It would be 2000 before the post of Keeper was re-classified as Director, when the traditional job titles, including those of the of post-war categories of Museum Assistant and Research Assistant, were discarded. The post of Director of the National Galleries was re-named Director-General.

The advisory committee continued to play what many considered an important role over the next three decades, looking carefully at potential acquisitions on points of historical detail and emphasising that the Portrait Gallery, though a repository of many wonderful works of art, was primarily concerned with the history of Scotland. In that period it would have many distinguished members, including John, Marquess of Bute, John Imrie, Keeper of the Records of Scotland, John Hume, architectural and industrial historian, Gordon Donaldson, the professor of Scottish History in the University of Edinburgh, the art historian Martin Kemp, and Christopher Smout, social historian and another Historiographer Royal. In 1986, however, the life of this committee was brought to an end, along with similar committees for the Gallery of Modern Art and the National Gallery. This stemmed, at least in part, from the National Heritage Act (Scotland) of 1985, which severed the close link with government, with funding by parliamentary vote being replaced by a grant-in-aid system. The number of trustees was increased from seven to twelve and a new management structure was introduced. It was the trustees' view that the committees had not been abolished but would continue as staff committees. They also recognised, they said, the value placed by the Keepers of both the Portrait Gallery and the Gallery of Modern Art on co-opted advisors (the National Gallery was not included in this equation) and left the option open to the two Keepers as to whether they should seek co-opted members. However, it was emphasised that they would advise the Keepers, not the Board. The option was never taken up.

All of this marked a swing back towards a more centralised National Galleries of Scotland. In many respects the advisory committee of the Portrait Gallery had been a more intellectually vigorous body than the Board, and its independence of mind may not have been to their taste. It might also be speculated that its removal was regarded as a necessary step towards plans that would have seen the end of the Portrait Gallery in its traditional form and its removal from its dedicated building. This was perhaps the most extraordinary episode in the later history of the Portrait Gallery. Such were the passions aroused in both public and private places, and exposed with varying degrees of accuracy in the press, that it is unlikely that the narrative that follows will match everyone's recollection of the course of events or the perceived motivation of those most closely involved. It is a story that stretches roughly over the years 1987 to 1994. As we have seen, the National Galleries had been cut loose from their long dependence on Scottish Office (latterly overseen by the Department of Education rather than the Home Department) in 1987, and were given a large degree of independence (the department still insisted on sending an observer to Board meetings, however).

The following year the department published a 'Policy Review and Financial Management Survey' of the Galleries. It asked the trustees 'to put in hand a radical review of their artistic policy'. While agreeing 'that the arrangement of the … collections is properly a matter for the discretion of the Trustees' (the kind of language that when used by civil servants often means the opposite), it went on to state: 'I [the senior civil servant who drafted the report] nevertheless take the view that the case for a Scottish [the radical new concept] Gallery (drawing largely on existing resources) should be aired with the aim of ensuring that the provision made by National Galleries of Scotland reflects the aspiration of visitors ….' This 'aspiration' appears to have been assumed rather than led by evidence. The view was repeated that the trustees 'might give particular attention to the case for a Scottish Gallery' and also consider 'the future role of a Portrait Gallery'. The use of the indefinite article in this last phrase was ominous.

This Policy Review is probably the spark that lit the undergrowth. At any rate, the trustees, under a new chairman, the merchant banker Angus Grossart, and with a new Director in place, Timothy Clifford, began to run with the idea. 'The Scottish Gallery' notion was fleshed into a 'Gallery of Scottish Art' over the next couple of years, but while many were pleased to see Scottish art being taken more seriously, many others, particularly Duncan Macmillan, author of a number of influential works on the subject, did not want to see that art confined in a 'ghetto': Scottish art was part of European art and should be displayed alongside it. Whatever the rights and wrongs of that argument, the whole matter burst into flames – and many were scorched – when it was realised that the core of the proposed gallery was to be the Portrait Gallery's Scottish pictures; and, worse still, in the popular mind at least, was the statement that the trustees 'would no longer have a use for the Findlay building'. The intention, at this stage – and the scenario would soon change dramatically – was to erect an entirely new gallery at the Dean Centre, costing, on some estimates, £21 million. A feasibility study was set in train, with funding of £50,000 from Scottish Office. With hindsight this funding seems odd, for as public opposition to the concept became more raucous, Scottish Office began to distance itself from the project and suggest that the trustees were moving ahead without their approval. It is probably fair to say that the trustees had not reckoned with the degree of affection that the Portrait Gallery had accrued over the years, nor with the opposition its demise (and especially the loss of the Findlay building) would provoke. But the situation was about to become far more complicated. If Scotland was to have a new National Gallery, should it necessarily be sited in Edinburgh? The City of Glasgow sensed an opportunity and the Director of its Art Gallery and Museum, Julian Spalding, who had earlier been rather dismissive of the whole idea, came forward with the offer of the city's Scottish pictures as a component of the new gallery – as long as it was sited in Glasgow. This was a highly attractive proposition, and by the autumn of 1993 Glasgow District Council had seized on the idea. The Glasgow Development Agency appointed an executive to 'assemble its package to win this grand project' (a package that would cost in the region of £100,000). Their proposals were quickly on the table. A riverbank site at

Kelvingrove was offered and architects Norman Foster and Terry Farrell produced contrasting preliminary designs. There was opposition within the Glasgow community to the loss of any part of that great public park, however, and the disused Sheriff Court in Ingram Street, a classical building of distinction, was offered as an alternative. Inevitably, the situation deteriorated into classic Edinburgh/Glasgow rivalry and the more essential aspects of the argument tended to be overlooked. Ultimately, the trustees had to make a decision about the gallery's location and it was not to be an easy one, either for them or their Director. The die was cast on 30 November, however, and the Glasgow *Evening Times* was able to announce with glee, under a headline 'That's just Capital', that Glasgow 'today won the bitter battle for the new £25 million Gallery of Scottish Art'.

Concern in many quarters, both east and west, for the continuance of the Portrait Gallery now gained momentum and was not allayed by assurances from the Director of the National Galleries early in December that 'We are not destroying the National Portrait Gallery. We are moving the collection to Glasgow and creating a new super portrait gallery.' This coincided with the first of two developments, both of which were to be unlike anything else in the history of the Gallery. It was announced that the Earl of Perth, long involved in the museum world, had secured a debate in the House of Lords, 'To ask Her Majesty's Government whether the proposed dismantling of the Scottish National Portrait Gallery will be fully considered before any action is taken.' The second of these unprecedented events was the calling of a public meeting by the Saltire Society to discuss the ramifications of what the trustees were proposing. The Society, a body concerned with Scottish culture and identity, was fiercely opposed to the trustees' plans.

This meeting took place in the Edinburgh College of Art on a cold, wet evening in mid-January 1994. So many turned up – well over 1,000 – that the discussion in the lecture theatre had to be relayed to an overflow audience in the sculpture court. The panel was chaired by Paul Scott, a greatly respected figure in the nationalist community. That the argument had by this time moved beyond the Glasgow/ Edinburgh divide was evident from the case made for the retention of the Portrait Gallery in its present form by the novelist Alasdair Gray, someone deeply identified with Glasgow. This was also the overwhelming feeling of the vast majority of those present (described by one journalist, who would later become a trustee, as the 'Jenners tearoom brigade').

The debate in the House of Lords on 26 January was extraordinary in a more sedate way, lasting from 7.54 pm to 10.55 pm (as volume 551 of the official report meticulously records). In the course of the evening there were contributions from nineteen peers, including maiden speeches by Lord Bruntsfield and Baroness Willoughby de Eresby. The contributions to the debate can be analysed in many ways – and they were – but what stands out is the fact that of the nineteen peers, fourteen opposed the 'dismantling' of the Portrait Gallery.

These startling, even historic, events, arousing passions some compared to those generated by the Disruption of the Church of Scotland in 1843, were, however, punctuation marks, and they decided nothing. In the background stood the figure of the Secretary of State for Scotland, Ian Lang, to whom the Portrait Gallery building would revert in the event of the trustees quitting it. It became increasingly obvious that he was dismayed by how the matter was being dealt with. At the same time, the barrage of criticism only increased, with contributions in the press from figures as diverse as the Duke of Buccleuch, Malcolm Rifkind (then Defence Secretary), Christopher Smout, Kenneth Hudson (a writer on museology over many years), the architectural historian Gavin Stamp (who considered the Portrait Gallery 'a special and wonderful place') and Lady Rosebery, a former trustee.

Soon it became clear that the trustees had given ground and were considering how the Portrait Gallery could be retained without the loss of their wider objective. This 'reappraisal' was not to the liking of the Director who was quoted in the March issue of *Country Life*, in the course of an interview with Michael Hall, as saying that the removal of the Portrait Gallery's collection from the planned gallery 'tears the guts out of the scheme'. The denouement came soon afterwards. On 9 May Ian Lang announced that he was not willing to back the trustees' proposals for a Gallery of Scottish Art in their present form. He did not entirely shut the door on the trustees' plans, however, and they would go on to pursue a different version of their original concept.

Lang's statement accepted the trustees' contention that the National Galleries had an accommodation problem, on which many of their arguments were predicated, and he indicated that he would be willing to give priority to the refurbishment of both the Royal Scottish Academy building, enabling it to be used for major exhibitions, and of the Portrait Gallery building when it was vacated by the National Museums of Scotland [79]. It is against this background that the most recent chapter in the history of the Portrait Gallery should be seen. Even as the above events were unfolding, the much dreamed-of new home for the Museum of Antiquities was at last taking shape in Chambers Street. Now merged with the Royal Museum of Scotland under a newly constituted board (a result of the Heritage Act of 1985 when the Board of the National Galleries gave up their residual responsibility for the Museum of Antiquities), the newly named Museum of Scotland opened in its iconic building in 1998, rather more than a hundred years after the Antiquaries had taken up residence in Findlay's building [80]. As the new museum opened, the Royal Scottish Academy closed (the last major exhibition of that era to be shown there in 1997 being the Portrait Gallery's *The Art of Sir Henry Raeburn*). The renovation of the Royal Scottish Academy building was to be a much more ambitious project than that envisaged at the time of Ian Lang's announcement, and involved not only the reconfiguration of the building itself, but the provision of new accommodation below street level, encompassing an elaborate link with the National Gallery [81]. This work, which cost some £27 million, was completed in 2003. The precedence given to work at the Mound inevitably delayed the redevelopment of the Queen Street building, but it was now a commitment of the new Board of Trustees.

Yet, although the National Museums of Scotland (now National Museums Scotland) had so substantially enlarged their estate in Edinburgh, their withdrawal

79 Museum of
Antiquities, *c.*1900
© RCAHMS
(Henry Bedford
Lemere Collection)

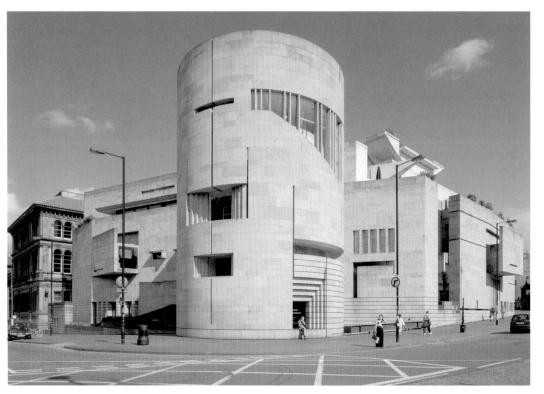

80 National
Museum of
Scotland
© Crown Copyright
RCAHMS

from the Queen Street building was far from immediate. A nod to the future had been the surrender, as early as 1990, of the small rooms on the ground floor of the east wing which were used to create a café, later enlarged by the addition of the north-east bay of the ground-floor gallery. Areas of that gallery were then ceded piecemeal, followed by the offices on the mezzanine level and upper floor of the east wing. This was followed by the Antiquaries' Library on the top floor, which the Portrait Gallery was then able to use as a rather rudimentary lecture theatre. However, both the northern section of the top floor and the entire first floor, given over to storage, were retained until the end. That end came in the spring of 2009 when both the remnants of the Museum and the entire Portrait Gallery quit the building prior to complete refurbishment. What Findlay had envisaged and others had modified (and even threatened) has come to pass, with the Scottish National Portrait Gallery triumphantly housed in the whole of Robert Rowand Anderson's great building.

81 The Weston Link connecting the Scottish National Gallery to the Royal Scottish Academy, completed in 2003

CHAPTER SIX

THE DEVELOPMENT
OF COLLECTING POLICIES

82 *Self-Portrait*
by Sir David Wilkie,
1804–5
Presented by J. Rankin
in 1898, P G 573

IT has been a commonplace in discussions of portrait galleries that the value of a portrait lies in the identity of the subject and that its qualities as a work of art are a secondary matter. Yet the works themselves are products of the human imagination and can never become mere substitutes for the person who has been portrayed. It goes without saying that the portrait should contain information about how the person looked, the accuracy of which tends to be taken for granted, but the context in which it was produced – its purpose, the expectations of whoever commissioned it, the convention in which the artist worked – must contribute to what it is. There is also that unique interchange between the maker of the portrait and the individual portrayed, where the 'object' becomes a subject. These are all factors that contribute to the meaning of the complex thing that a portrait is, and are part of the distinguishing aura that gives it a unique place in time and history. In that sense it has become a relic, where authenticity is everything and the viewer is momentarily in a presence. Underlying how this response is evoked, of course, is that other mysterious layer, the aesthetic dimension, which takes the imprint of the intensity that the artist's unique gift brings to his or her task. It is something that was expressed in forthright terms by James Caw in the earliest days of the Portrait Gallery, when the collection was in its infancy and he was trying to envisage how it would develop. Giving evidence to a government departmental committee inquiry into the affairs of the Board of Manufactures in 1903/4, he remarked: 'Of course, the Treasury has always been telling the London people [those in charge of the National Portrait Gallery] that they are not for good pictures, but for portraits of people, but you cannot have good portraits without having good pictures.' Caw was clearly aware that while portraits can be used for their informational content, or as parts of a narrative, there were deeper issues that portrait galleries must not lose sight of. If they do, the label will take precedence over the work of art – a situation that has been seen to become a danger confronting all didactic picture galleries of whatever kind.

Nevertheless, the collecting policies of portrait galleries have always been easier to define than those of galleries dedicated to the history of painting. The latter were often formed from amorphous pre-existing collections, such as nationalised royal collections or gifts that provided a foundation for something more varied. Even where they were consciously formed as fulfilment of a national need to illustrate the schools of painting of the past, they were constantly being modified and re-defined. Portrait galleries however, at least in the early stages of development, were not concerned with the history of art but had a single, more clearly determined aim – a national history.

Throughout the greater part of their nineteenth- and twentieth-century existence the National Portrait Gallery in London and the Scottish National Portrait Gallery in Edinburgh built up their collections in similar ways, on the basis of the injunctions of the various Victorian statesmen and sages, especially Carlyle, who had been instrumental in their foundation. Clearly, there was no problem in seeing Scottish history as something distinct from English history; but how separate was Scottish history from British history in the period when portraits were commonplace? In time the London gallery would acquire portraits of notable Scots like Robert Burns and Walter Scott, presumably because they were seen as part of British literature, but the acquisition by the Edinburgh gallery of a portrait of, say, William Wordsworth, would always have been highly unlikely – even given his Romantic journeys into Scotland and his admiration for Burns. Yet, in 1925, the Edinburgh Portrait Gallery bought a Roubiliac terracotta bust of John Milton – was it sneaked in because it was a beautiful object in itself, or was it because of his influence on the fabricator of Ossian's remains, James Macpherson?

Monarchs, of course, and near-monarchs like the Stuart princes, were more straightforward and their images were happily acquired by both institutions, usually without a hint of conflict. On rare occasions, however, the Scottish gallery would make a sally into territory that was manifestly British – for example, by accepting the gift in 1930 of nineteen portraits by James Guthrie of statesmen who had played a vital role in the First World War and its aftermath, where many of the subjects were English, Welsh, Canadian or South African. This 'British' aspiration was underlined by the purchase in that climactic year, 1945, of Guthrie's compositional sketch for the vast group portrait, *Statesmen of the Great War*, for which the nineteen individual portraits had been studies. Guthrie's great paean of praise to these statesmen, now in the National Portrait Gallery in London, had also, like the group of nineteen studies, been a gift to the nation in 1930 (though by a different donor), and the coincidence of dates suggests that at that time there was an urge towards a cohesive Britishness.

These kinds of boundaries have never, however, been formally defined and indeed they have scarcely even been looked at – perhaps there was an unwillingness to disturb a political hornet's nest. From the point of view of actual acquisition there has been little disagreement, though curators may from time to time have cast an envious eye on what their counterparts had acquired. Although there was no competition at the time, no doubt the two full-length portraits by Gabriel Blanchet of the young Stuart princes, Charles and Henry Benedict (two of the artist's finest paintings which grace the National Portrait Gallery in London) stirred the acquisitive instincts of later curators in Edinburgh. However, the question of overlap has always been dealt with in a very informal fashion.

As the Edinburgh collection grew, a 'national' feature became more and more evident, something that did not apply to the same degree in London. This was the realisation that elements of the collection, besides illustrating Scottish history, also played an important role in the history of Scottish art – a painting, for example, like David Wilkie's beautiful early self-portrait [82], painted while still under the influence of the broad, planar manner of Raeburn, and equal to anything being painted in Europe. This awareness may also have been the result of the Portrait Gallery being part of that bigger whole, the National Galleries of Scotland, where the National Gallery had a specific commitment to illustrate the history of Scottish art. It was this that led in 1983 to a decision that the collecting policy should be extended to include portraits on the grounds that, although the subject had no particular significance in Scottish history, the work of art could be defined as a landmark in the history of Scottish portraiture. It was this policy that led to the purchase in 1983 of Allan Ramsay's portrait of his first wife Anne Bayne, whose brief life ended in childbirth in 1743 [83]. The unique mixture of grace and realism in this portrait shows Ramsay at an important turning point in his life, before he

83 *Anne Ramsay (née Bayne)* by Allan Ramsay, about 1739
Bought in 1983, PG 2603

went on to make his unique contribution to both British and European painting. It might be argued that the painting should have found its place in the Scottish collection at the National Gallery, but demarcation lines were kept fluid and its acquisition also marked a growing interest in the whole concept of portraiture per se. A further reflection of this policy was the decision about the same time to collect as complete a set of James Tassie's vitreous portrait medallions as possible. The collection had already acquired a strong interest in Tassie through the bequest of a large body of his material by his nephew, William Tassie, to the Board of Manufactures in 1860. (This included three sets of his 15,000 or so reproductions of classical gemstones – an anomaly in terms of collecting, display, and housing, that has never been resolved.) The portrait medallions, though often of historically important individuals (Adam Smith is uniquely portrayed by Tassie), also portray many obscure individuals, but are so redolent of their time in so many different ways – a kind of sculptural counterpart to Raeburn's depiction of his own society – that it is surprising they are not better known [84].

84 *Adam Smith* by James Tassie, 1787 Bought in 1886, PG 157

Another departure from more traditional policies came about the same time, when it was decided that topographical paintings, where the informational content was high, and paintings that were veristic descriptions of important historical events, should also be acquired. Part of this thinking was the simple one that no other gallery or museum in Scotland (although it might conceivably have been a function of the National Museums of Scotland) was especially interested in this kind of material. Yet the case could easily be made for a gallery whose prime – even founding – aim was to illustrate Scottish history; in addition, material of this sort often had strong personalised references. Hence the acquisition of Alexander Keirincx's painting, *Falkland Palace and the Howe of Fife* [85], one of a series of Scottish views commissioned by Charles I, probably soon after his triumphal entry into Edinburgh in 1633 as King of Scots. This was followed by the acquisition in 1986 of another of these views by Keirincx, *Seton Palace and the Firth of Forth Estuary*, a depiction of a building with other profound historical resonances.

85 *Falkland Palace and the Howe of Fife* by Alexander Keirincx, about 1639 Bought in 1977, PG 2409

86 *A View of Stornoway* by James Barret, 1798 Bought in 2002, PG 3291

The first steps in this new direction were taken in 1976 with the acquisition of two 'estate pictures', *Yester House* by an unidentified artist and *Taymouth Castle* by James Norie and Jan Griffier. The pictures had associations with the Hay of Yester and Campbell of Glenorchy families respectively and, perhaps more importantly, each illustrated in considerable detail the workings of man on the natural landscape. Other views with similar layers of meaning acquired under this policy have been *Edinburgh from Canonmills*, a view of about 1820 by the Glasgow artist John Knox, and *A View of Stornoway* by James Barret, the most recently purchased of this distinct group [86].

As with topographical paintings, there had already been some random acquisitions of paintings of historical events (not the concocted sort Carlyle had

dismissed out of hand) before this policy was officially adopted. There was, for instance, the small study known as *The Baptism of Prince Maurice of Battenberg* by George Ogilvy Reid, a record of an event at Balmoral Castle in 1891, the first baptism of a royal prince in Scotland for 300 years (the final painting is now in the royal collection). However, although an illustration of a historical event, it has a substantial portrait content, including the baby's parents, the elderly Queen Victoria who holds the child for the minister's blessing, and many others. Closer to pure narrative is the depiction of *The Battle of Glenshiel* by Peter Tillemans [87], acquired in 1984. (Amusingly, though not for the curators concerned, it was originally believed, on the strength of Christie's expertise, to represent the Battle of Killiecrankie, and was bought as such.) It is a painting that is both topographical and an illustration of a little-known episode in Jacobite history in 1719 – and probably as close as a portrait gallery can get to that near mythical figure, Rob Roy McGregor. It also includes verifiable portraits of Lord George Murray and General Joseph Wightman. However, there is no portrait content in the most recently acquired of these historical narratives, *The German Fleet after Surrender* by James Paterson [88], a painting where the Portrait Gallery departs furthest from its more traditional role as a pantheon of the great (and sometimes the less than good). All of this said, since galleries and museums are often riddled with anomalies, a view, *Edinburgh from the West*, showing the national fortress on its rock, had been silently acquired as far back as 1929, bequeathed by the former Secretary to the Board of Manufactures, Alexander Inglis.

PORTRAITS OF THE LIVING

The most dramatic new departure to the collecting policy came in 1982 when the trustees agreed that portraits of the living could be acquired. Although never quite spelled out, there had always been a tacit fear that politicians and other members of the establishment might take advantage of their social position to ensure that what they perceived as their important role in national history would be marked by the inclusion of their portrait in the national collection. This fear that the historical record might be manipulated was real enough and still has to be taken account of today. The policy of excluding the living, however, was likely to have an unfortunate outcome: opportunities of acquiring images of undoubtedly significant figures might be missed. There was also the fact that visitors had an appetite for portraits of famous living people in an age of celebrity. Yet, what seemed at the time to be a radical development had in fact been adumbrated from the very beginning of the Portrait Gallery's history, and was a spectre that would occasionally raise its head over the years without ever being fully resolved. As early as January 1887, Lord Lothian had written to fellow committee member Fettes Douglas on the need of 'admitting Portraits of living persons', a theme he was still pursuing a couple of years later. Lothian's arguments were the quite reasonable ones, that, unlike portraits of those long dead, there would never be any doubt over the identities of both subject and artist. Fettes Douglas evidently did not agree with the proposition, and wrote to the Board, with his usual nice use of language, 'You know my

87 *The Battle of Glenshiel 10 June 1719* by Peter Tillemans, 1719

Bought with the assistance of the National Heritage Memorial Fund and the Art Fund in 1984, P G 2635

88 *The German Fleet after Surrender, Firth of Forth, 21 November 1918* by James Paterson, 1918

Bought in 1988, P G 2733

general views there anent'. At about the same time, John Miller Gray prepared a memorandum on commissioning portraits of contemporaries and seems to have jumped the gun with a scheme that he said was already underway. This was to commission pencil drawings of fifty subjects, apparently on his own initiative. He was negotiating with the publisher Constable to produce 300 folios of facsimiles of these drawings, the originals of which he would then give to the gallery. He added a note on 'sitters who have already consented', but for some reason left their names out, so that it remains unclear if anything was achieved.

The subject did not raise its head again until June 1909 when the Board discussed a 'Proposal', presumably from Caw, 'to commission Portraits of Living Persons'. There seems to have been an unwillingness on the part of the Board to grasp the nettle of commissioning, for the matter was deferred or continued at three subsequent meetings. At the final meeting of the year the topic resurfaced but in an entirely different form, with Caw submitting a schedule drawn up by himself and John Ritchie Findlay which was 'to be sent out with a view to obtaining particulars of Portraits which might ultimately be of interest to the Portrait Gallery'. Evidently the idea of commissioning portraits of the living had been dropped and the word 'ultimately' implies that the tacit proscription on including living subjects was being reinforced.

Much later, in 1931, progress was made by the inauguration of 'a scheme whereby a series of photographs of distinguished living persons was made available for the purpose of establishing a permanent record of such persons for future reference …'. These were the work of the Edinburgh portrait photographer Edward Drummond Young [77, 78]. They were not, however, to be regarded as part of the main collection, as the phrase 'for future reference' indicates, and clearly the scheme suffered from the hierarchies of the time (still not entirely abandoned) where painting was deemed a superior category to photography. There is an amusing record of some of the subjects of these photographs creeping into the Print Room to have their images taken out for viewing.

In the mid-1930s there is the first mention of what in effect was a ruse to acquire portraits of the living. This involved the Modern Arts Association under the presidency of the collector and critic Arthur Kay. At the unveiling of a bust of Lady Margaret Sackville by Pittendrigh Macgillivray, Kay remarked that 'it was one of the peculiarities of the modern arrangement that no portraits were allowed to pass into the national collection until the sitters had gone far away from us; and therefore the Modern Arts Association had, in one or two cases, accepted trusteeship of works of art which were worthy of passing into the collection of the nation'. This arrangement was used on a number of occasions: for example, two portraits of Ramsay Macdonald were acquired in 1938 (the year after his death) by this route, the painting by Ambrose McEvoy [89] and the bronze bust by Jacob Epstein.

Presumably because of the disordered nature of the times, the 'distinguished contemporaries' scheme of the photographer Drummond Young was suspended at the beginning of the Second World War. The scheme was not to be revived, and the whole subject became quiescent until the offer in 1955 of a large group of portrait

drawings by David Foggie from the artist's widow. The trustees accepted these splendid drawings with alacrity but someone noticed that they 'included some of living persons'. This was perceived as a real stumbling block and of the original thirty-eight, only twenty-four were accepted, all presumed to be safely dead – in fact, the drawing of the philosopher Norman Kemp Smith, still with three years of his life to run, somehow crept past their scrutiny. (The remainder, some still alive, including the novelist Compton Mackenzie, were accepted in 1962.) This quandary roused the Board to action and the Keeper, Robin Hutchison (himself the son of an eminent society portrait painter), was asked to look into the rule that excluded the living. The issue was referred to the Secretary to the Board who, after researching the matter, concluded that it was 'clear from the information available that any rule … was self-imposed by the Board … and that they may therefore rescind this rule'. It was, in effect, not a rule but a convention – but one that would persist for more than another two decades.

This indecision stretching over more than half a century went hand in hand with the decay of what has been called the great tradition in portraiture, where there was a growing divergence between portraiture and the evolving arts of the time. There was also an increasing reliance on the new technology of photography in the second half of the nineteenth century, which seemed to question the traditional suppositions of artists. The dialectic, or interplay, between these developments would lead in the first half of the twentieth century to the art of portraiture falling into disrepute, a situation exacerbated by the swing of fashion against figurative art. The outcome tended to be twofold: many historically interesting people were simply not portrayed or relied on an anodyne form of portraiture that aped the tonalities of studio photography – in essence the 'boardroom' portrait, where little was asked for and little was given. Change on both fronts beckoned, however. In the years that followed the Second World War, artists in Britain such as Francis Bacon, Graham Sutherland and Lucian Freud returned to the human figure in a way that, although profoundly modern in feeling, took account of the art of the past. (They had counterparts in France, such as Francis Gruber and Alberto Giacometti.) As far as portraiture was concerned, Sutherland was particularly important. His portrait of Somerset Maugham of 1948 lent his idiosyncratic landscape forms to the depiction of a specific human being and seemed entirely new. It raised many eyebrows. Sutherland would go on to paint a dozen or so portraits in an idiom that many found strange at the time, particularly Lady Churchill who ultimately ordered the destruction of the artist's portrait of her husband. It could be claimed that with these portraits Sutherland changed the whole evolution of portrait painting – yet at no time would he have accepted the designation 'portrait painter'.

At the same time, the growing realisation that many significant figures in contemporary history were likely to depart the scene unportrayed led in 1973 to the National Portrait Gallery in London making a radical shift in policy and starting to collect portraits of the living, many of them commissioned. In 1982 the Scottish National Portrait Gallery followed suit, when the trustees agreed to commission a portrait of the Queen Mother. Given the great popularity of the subject it was an uncontroversial choice. The choice of artist was rather different, and points to a distinctive aspect of the Portrait Gallery's commissioning policy that has by and large continued. With the support of the advisory committee, it was agreed that the artists chosen to carry out the commissions should be, within certain perceptual limits, representative of a broad swathe of contemporary art, artists who would make portraits that were redolent of the art of their own time – a quality that any good portrait should possess.

The artist chosen to paint the Queen Mother was Avigdor Arikha, an Israeli painter long settled in Paris, who was astonished to be asked to carry out the

commission, something that he had never done before [90]. He was a figurative painter who virtually eschewed style, so that his faintly disturbing and oblique art was difficult to classify. Portraits of his friends and family made it clear that 'likeness' in the conventional sense was well within his range and the risk was taken. In the event he established a close relationship with the Queen Mother. Paradoxically, given the new direction that the Portrait Gallery believed it was pursuing, it was Arikha's friend the writer Samuel Beckett who urged him to accept the commission as it was 'part of the great tradition'. Arikha would go on to

90 *Elizabeth the Queen Mother* by Avigdor Arikha, 1983

Commissioned by the Scottish National Portrait Gallery in 1982, PG 2598

91 Mick McGahey
by Maggi Hambling,
1988

Commissioned by
the Scottish National
Portrait Gallery in 1988,
PG 2747

paint two other distinguished portraits for the collection: a three-quarter length
of Alec Douglas Home (a landmark in contemporary portraiture, as Sutherland's
of Somerset Maugham had been), and a double portrait of Ludovic Kennedy
and Moira Shearer. Other artists who followed in the next two decades included
Sandy Moffat (Muriel Spark), John Wonnacott (Adam Thomson, founder of British
Caledonian Airways), Humphrey Ocean (Danny McGrain, footballer), Maggi
Hambling (Mick McGahey) [91], Patrick Heron (Jo Grimond) [92], Jack Knox (a
self-portrait – he was a trustee at the time), John Bellany (Peter Maxwell Davies)
and Adrian Wiszniewski (a portrait of the three directors of the Citizens Theatre).

Among more recent portraits commissioned, or purchased, in the same vein, are Jennifer McRae's portraits of the novelist Robin Jenkins and the broadcaster Kirsty Wark [93]. The latter, simple in form and completely contemporary, has the intensity, and profundity, of the great Flemish portraits of the fifteenth century. Another remarkable recent commission has been Ken Currie's *Three Oncologists*, an emotionally encompassing triple portrait of three cancer surgeons in the University of Dundee in their surgical environment [94]. It is a painting where the artist has solved the perennial problem of relating more than two figures in a portrait with a subtlety that is Rembrandtesque – as is its overwhelming emotional intensity.

When the project to commission portraits of the living got underway, and for many years afterwards, the choice of both subject and artist was a curatorial one – a marked difference from the situation in the National Portrait Gallery in London where trustees were deeply involved in the decisions on suitable subjects. This is a curiosity, for it is not clear why professional curatorial decisions, taken with professional advice, on who is an appropriate subject, should not suffice in the same way as the choice of artist. If, however, the choice of subject were seen as a means of conveying an honour, then the position would be quite different. There is certainly an issue here, and the political, social agenda that was feared in the early history of portrait galleries has not entirely gone away. In due course, the

92 *Joseph Grimond, 1st Baron Grimond* by Patrick Heron, 1987
Commissioned by the Scottish National Portrait Gallery in 1985, PG 2717

93 *Kirsty Wark* by Jennifer McRae, 2002
Bought in 2005, PG 3396

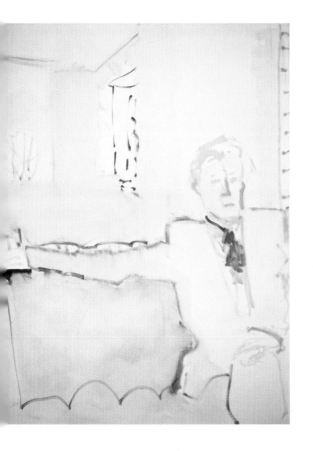

94 *Three Oncologists*
by Ken Currie, 2002

Commissioned by
the Scottish National
Portrait Gallery in 2002,
PG 3296

95 *Newhaven
Fishwives* (perhaps
Mrs Elizabeth
(Johnstone) Hall on
the right) by David
Octavius Hill and
Robert Adamson

Bought in 1975,
PGP HA 328

trustees in Scotland, while leaving the choice of artist with the curators, insisted on vetting lists of potential subjects, a system that has lent some credence to an underlying feeling that the Portrait Gallery was running some kind of alternative honours system.

PHOTOGRAPHY

Another important development at this time was a far greater emphasis on photography. The most obvious manifestation of this was the creation of the Scottish Photography Archive in 1984, a distinct though not separate section with its own Curator, Sara Stevenson (who would become a world authority on photography) and an assistant. Its creation was made possible by sponsorship from the oil company Mobil, an early example of the kind of business sponsorship that would become ever more important to the National Galleries of Scotland, though usually in the field of special exhibitions. The Portrait Gallery had long had what might be termed a subliminal interest in photography as an art form because

of the unparalleled collection of early Scottish photography that it had built up rather haphazardly, particularly the unrivalled group of around 700 images by the pioneers David Octavius Hill and Robert Adamson. Initially these were acquired because of their portrait content, though many also depicted ordinary life, particularly the fisherfolk of the Firth of Forth, and were probably perceived as little more than factual records [95]. However, with time their aesthetic value, and the significance of Hill and Adamson in the history of world photography, became more and more apparent. In the early 1980s other important groups of material by early Scottish photographers were added to the collection, often as a result of gifts, as the Gallery's commitment to the art form began to act as a magnet. Among them

96 *At Auchmithie* by James Cox, 1881
Bought in 1983,
PGP 37, vol.7.32

97 *Boatmen on the River Volga* by William Carrick, 1875
Bought in 1984,
PGP 44.1

98 *Sir John Buchan, 1st Baron Tweedsmuir* by Yousuf Karsh, 1937
Presented by the photographer in 1985,
PGP 95.1

were photographs by Thomas Keith, Robert McPherson, James Cox [96], John Muir Wood, Joseph Forrester (active in Portugal) and William Carrick (working in Russia). [97]

On this historical foundation the Photography Archive, initially conceived as a resource centre collecting information on other collections of photography and offering advice in areas like conservation, quickly moved into the orbit of contemporary Scottish photography, encompassing work ranging from what might be termed conventional to startlingly innovative works, such as those of Calum Colvin. In time the word Archive came to be seen as mildly misleading and in 1996, in recognition of how the section had expanded, and of its aspirations, it was renamed the Scottish National Photography Collection. Recently plans were afoot to create a new Centre for Scottish Photography in the old Royal High School building – a building a mere stone's throw from D.O. Hill's Rock House on Calton Hill where he and Adamson had virtually created modern photography. It was

99 *Sir William Gillies* by Lida Moser, 1949
Bought in 1984, PGP 43.3

envisaged that this would have encompassed the collections, or part of them, that had been built up by the Portrait Gallery, but for a whole variety of reasons the notion has so far foundered.

This dedication to photography also encompassed a regular series of special exhibitions that looked at a wide range of the art form. Even before the original archive had been founded, there had been shows of work by photographers like Jane Bown, Bill Brandt and Karsh of Ottawa – all three curated by the National Portrait Gallery in London. A surprising spin-off from the Karsh exhibition was the artist's gift to the Portrait Gallery of two photographs of the novelist John Buchan, one in native American headgear [98]. Two other notable exhibitions were devoted to the work of the Canadian Lida Moser and the American Annie Leibovitz. Moser was something of a discovery (the exhibition was curated by the late W. Gordon Smith) – but really a re-discovery, for, as a young *Vogue*

photographer, she had visited Scotland in 1949 to photograph the leading lights of the Scottish cultural renaissance [99]. The Leibovitz show resulted in two other gifts, an image of the actor Sean Connery [100] and the famous photograph of John Lennon with Yoko Ono. These photographs demonstrate how the nature of the collection had evolved, under curatorial pressure rather than as a result of a determined policy of the trustees – the Connery photograph unambiguously representing 'the greatest living Scot' and therefore a 'standard' Portrait Gallery acquisition, the Lennon/Ono photograph simply a startling example of a major American photographer.

A changing direction implied, though not yet determined, by these opposites, is a merging of what has been a Portrait Gallery collection with the collection of contemporary photography built up by the Gallery of Modern Art. This move towards something that still awaits a clear definition was marked in 2001 by the

100 *Sir Sean Connery* by Annie Leibovitz, 1993
Presented by the photographer in 1994, P G P 158.1

publication of *Photography in the National Galleries of Scotland*. This book contains a concise history of a collection that had grown to contain some 27,000 items, its range of subject matter unlike anything held by any other portrait gallery.

PHOTOGRAPHY AS RECORD

An entirely different form of photography has been a concern of the Portrait Gallery since the inter-war years. As in any gallery or museum in the twentieth century, collections of photographs for record and comparative purposes have grown ever more important. This particular 'photothèque', from random beginnings, was quite quickly systematised into a method of identifying portraits outside the gallery's own collection, wherever they were to be found, by both subject and artist. Just as the evolving use of the building was marked by the personality of Stanley Cursiter, so the indexing of photographs (and engravings) in what came to be known as the Reference Section was also initiated by him. Subdivided by nationality and periods of time, the photographs mounted and filed in drawers, much of the earlier work on this system was carried out by members of the warding staff who had demonstrated some interest in history, and later by clerks seconded from Scottish Office who quickly mastered the intricacies of the system. It was not until 1971 that this particular role was taken over by a research assistant with an academic background. The significance of this part of the gallery's work was soon emphasised by the appointment of an Assistant Keeper to take charge of this section and develop its potential. This essentially historical function is now performed by an archivist. From the very beginning an attempt was made to make this material available to the general public, but insufficient staff made, and continues to make, this aspiration difficult.

From the early 1950s a great deal of this photographic material resulted from photographic surveys of private collections in Scotland. This was set in train by Ellis Waterhouse during his brief period (1951–3) as Director of the National Galleries of Scotland – the same Ellis Waterhouse who famously found Scotland 'very Scottish'! His initiative was made possible in constrained financial circumstances by substantial financial help from the Frick Art Reference Library in New York, who benefited from the photographs and information they were able to add to their own records. These surveys took in virtually every painting in the private (occasionally institutional) collections concerned, but since the majority were usually portraits the system was largely run by Portrait Gallery staff. One difference from a similar exercise carried out by the Courtauld Institute of Art in London in the same years was that each item photographed was subject to some basic research, so that a brief catalogue of the collection was produced, rather than a mere list. This was of considerable benefit to the owners of the collections and contributed to the goodwill that had to be part of the agreement (which often involved considerable temporary disarrangement of the house concerned). This work resulted in an important record of art in Scottish country houses, valuable for scholars worldwide who from the beginning were allowed access to these riches. So much effort by Portrait Gallery staff went into this work that it might be thought that more time went into cataloguing these collections than was expended on the Portrait Gallery's own collection. Sadly, in 1992, a sign of more recent economic woes, the Frick had to withdraw its support. It remains to be seen if these surveys can continue.

Although this photographic archive was mainly used by art historians, often in conjunction with the Gallery's large holding of engravings, and also by those concerned with family history, there had always been an awareness that the images contained a great deal of information that would be of use to social historians and picture researchers working in the ever-expanding historical publication scene. It was for this reason that in 1978 the Keeper, Robin Hutchison, initiated what came to be known as the Social History Index. This involved the close scrutiny of these images and the listing of their contents under a variety of headings – clothes, jewellery, furniture, household items, for example, all placed in a chronological framework. It was a labour-intensive exercise – and literally endless – and much of the work was initially carried out by a team of volunteers under the direction of the curator, Rosalind Marshall, who managed what was variously termed the Archive, the Print Room or the Reference Section. Volunteers had begun to enter the gallery system in the early 1970s and their numbers increased considerably in the years that followed. Sometimes they were viewed with a certain degree of suspicion by the professional staff who feared dilution, and there were vague agreements that they should only carry out tasks peripheral to the main purposes of the Gallery. The Social History Index quickly became a central activity, especially as officialdom (that is, the civil service) came to see it as fulfilling some of the growing requirements of galleries and museums to be more accessible to the general public. Its value as an important educational resource was soon recognised in official publications, and little notice was taken of its reliance on volunteers. The vast amount of material recorded has not yet been digitised – and obviously when that comes it will be even more widely used.

CHAPTER SEVEN

THE COLLECTION

THE collection in its earliest days, and as it can be imagined on display in its pristine new building, was an extremely amorphous affair. Leaving aside items that were placed on loan, and consequently fluctuated in numbers over the years, it is a remarkable fact that of the first hundred items that were entered in the Portrait Gallery's acquisition register, once a proper record system had been put in train, seventy-nine were subsequently de-accessioned. These were images of people of such fame that there could be no argument that they were worthy of representation in the collection – Mary, Queen of Scots, later Stuart monarchs, the famous Jacobites, Adam Smith, David Hume, James Watt, Walter Scott, Robert Burns – and the great Thomas Carlyle himself, who had died only a few years earlier. However, all of these were plaster casts of coins and medals bearing portraits which had been given by the trustees of the British Museum. In time, they could not stand any rigorous test of authenticity, they were vulnerable to careless handling, and many would eventually be replaced by their original metal counterparts which, although multiples, could usually meet the criteria of having been cast in the sitter's lifetime, or close to it, and thus carry that aura essential to a truly historical portrait. As well as loans, portraits were both donated and bought in the period when the Portrait Gallery was under construction. Pride of place, Queen Street number 1 as it were (later rebranded 'P G 1' to avoid confusion with the registers of the Scottish National Gallery and the Scottish National Gallery of Modern Art) went to John Watson Gordon's portrait of the soldier Major-General Patrick Lindsay. This was a gift in 1884 from the Revd H.B. Sands, an Anglican clergyman living in Edinburgh and the first in a long line of donors. As was to be expected, there was no pattern to be discerned in these earliest acquisitions: a drawing by Stephen Poyntz Denning of John Burnet, famous as David Wilkie's engraver (given by the artist William Bell Scott); a secondary drawing of the poet Allan Ramsay (from the same source); the painter Francis Grant by J.P. Knight; the arctic explorer Admiral John Ross by B.R. Faulkener; and a beautiful panel portrait attributed to Robert Peake of Lady Arabella Stuart of 1605 [102]. These demonstrate the kind of diversity that would typify the collection throughout its history.

Leaving aside the subsequently de-accessioned reproductions of coins and medals, the earliest unquestionably major figures in Scottish history to enter the 'pantheon' were Walter Scott and Robert Burns, the former represented by an early drawing by Andrew Geddes (purchased in 1885), the latter by an ink silhouette by John Miers which, though a modest image, has become a minor icon [103]. In the same year, Scott would come to be represented by a romantic image of himself and his hounds at Abbotsford, painted by Francis Grant in 1831, the year before Scott's death, and bequeathed in 1885 by Lady Ruthven [104]. It would have

101 *Robert Burns* by Alexander Nasmyth, 1787
Bequeathed by Colonel William Burns to the Board of Manufactures in 1872 and transferred to the Scottish National Portrait Gallery, P G 1063

102 *Lady Arabella Stuart*
attributed to Robert Peake, 1605
Bought in 1884, PG 9

103 *Robert Burns* by John Miers, 1787
W.F. Watson Bequest in 1886, PG 113

seemed contemporary to those who took it into the Portrait Gallery only fifty or so years after the writer's death, in a way that we can no longer quite imagine. In time Burns would be represented by eleven more or less authentic portraits – the entire gamut – while Scott would merit over sixty, evidence of the social chasm that divided the two great writers.

The silhouette of Burns by Miers was one of a large number of portraits, mostly drawings and watercolours, bequeathed by the Edinburgh bookseller, William Finlay Watson. Of the first 150 items to be officially registered, some thirty came from Watson's bequest. Others from the same source, however, seem to have lain in some kind of limbo and were not treated as proper acquisitions until long afterwards – Allan Ramsay's drawing of Flora Macdonald, for example, was not registered as part of the primary collection until 1954. Similarly treated was a group of twenty-eight copy drawings of portraits (mostly authentic) by David Stewart Erskine, Earl of Buchan [2], begetter of the notion of the 'Caledonian Temple of Fame'. Another early bequest, again from Lady Ruthven, was Pompeo Batoni's portrait of the African explorer James Bruce, the first truly European masterpiece to enter the collection [105]. At the same time came the first purchases of vitreous paste portraits by James Tassie – a group of seven that included Hugh Blair, the inventor of literary criticism, and Andrew Lumisden, the one-time secretary to the Young Pretender, Charles Edward Stuart. No doubt stimulated by John Miller Gray's interest in Tassie and his nephew William, the Portrait Gallery would continue to seek portraits by Tassie over the years, replacing replica casts with originals whenever possible.

Another important source for the collection in its earliest days were the twenty-six historical portraits amassed by David Laing which he had bequeathed to the Society of Antiquaries of Scotland in 1878. Laing, as an early proponent of the

Portrait Gallery – indeed he had collected these portraits in the hope of such a gallery being founded – would have approved of their loan to the Portrait Gallery, especially as the Society's Museum had been ensconced in the same building since 1891. These loans included two important Scottish 'primitive' portraits, one of architect David Anderson, and the other of calligrapher Esther Kello [106]; and the strange double 'self-portrait' of Alexander Runciman with fellow artist John Brown, painted in 1784 [107]. Placed on loan by the Society at the same time were Brown's thirty-two large pencil drawings of various antiquarians and their associates. All of this material remained on loan into a third century when, in 2009, it was finally ceded to the Portrait Gallery.

104 *Sir Walter Scott and his Dogs* by Sir Francis Grant, 1831
Bequeathed by Lady Ruthven in 1885, PG 103

105 *James Bruce of Kinnaird* by Pompeo Batoni, 1762
Bequeathed by Lady Ruthven in 1885, PG 141

106 *Esther Kello* by an unknown artist, 1595
Gifted by the Society of Antiquaries of Scotland to the Scottish National Portrait Gallery in 2009, PG 3556

107 *Alexander Runciman and John Brown* by the subjects, 1784
Gifted by the Society of Antiquaries of Scotland in 2009, PG 3545

It might also have been expected that the thirty-four portraits which comprised the first room in the Scottish National Gallery when it opened its doors in 1859 would come to the new Portrait Gallery. This 'proto-portrait gallery' had been formed quite deliberately as the foundation on which it was hoped that a national collection of historical portraits could be built. It was a reflection of the thoughts of people like David Laing himself, and, of course, Thomas Carlyle. It was an odd collection, however, that hardly matched their views. Nearly half were portraits of artists, most of whom had hardly become historical figures, and others were of men who had been instrumental in the founding of the National Gallery. A number were loans from the Royal Scottish Academy, including a self-portrait of William Aikman, and Raeburn's spectacular portrait of Mrs Scott Moncrieff. Neither of these would ever come to the Portrait Gallery (indeed, it had bought another equally good self-portrait by Aikman in 1886). Ramsay's famous portrait of David Hume was also included in this early showing, having been given to the National Gallery the year prior to its opening. It eventually reached the Portrait Gallery in the mid-1920s when a large number of items were transferred, presumably because by this time its aesthetic qualities were considered to be outweighed by its historical value [109]. Aikman's portrait of the English poet John Gay – an anomaly, of course – did make its way to Queen Street much earlier, in 1910, when the Gallery benefited from the new relationship with the Royal Scottish Academy which ceded most of its historical collection, including some twenty portraits, to the National Galleries of Scotland in exchange for its new premises in the Royal Institution building.

A significant transfer from the National Gallery did take place early in 1889 when preparations were being made for the opening of the fledgling Gallery. The

Board of Manufactures agreed on a list of fifteen paintings, two busts, one statue, and twelve medallions, that 'In view of the approaching opening of the National Portrait Gallery in the New Building in Queen Street', should be transferred from the National Gallery. There was, however, one major bone of contention and that was the famous portrait of Robert Burns by Alexander Nasmyth [101]. This had been bequeathed in 1872 to the Board of Manufactures as trustees 'of the Scottish National Gallery' by the poet's son Colonel William Burns. Those trustees who did not approve of the transfer relied heavily on what they perceived to be a legal restriction in the wording of the bequest. Since the matter had not been resolved at their meeting, the Secretary to the Board, Alexander Inglis, prepared a printed memorandum setting out both sides of the argument and requested a written response from each trustee. Their replies, received during April and May, were annotated by Inglis, For and Against. The arguments nearly all touched on the perennial problem of 'art' versus 'portrait'. Those voting for the transfer included, perhaps inevitably, a number of those closely associated with the Portrait Gallery, including Noël Paton, Fettes Douglas, Lord Lothian, and Findlay. Noël Paton, referring to the painting as 'the Burns Icon' – an early use, or misuse, of the term – was particularly adamant on 'the paramount Claim which the National Portrait Gallery has'. Findlay (writing from Cannes) delivered what might have seemed the

108 *Self-portrait* by Allan Ramsay, about 1756
Presented by the Royal Scottish Academy in 1910, PG 727

109 *David Hume* by Allan Ramsay
Bequeathed by Mrs Macdonald Hume to the Scottish National Gallery in 1858 and transferred to the Scottish National Portrait Gallery, PG 1057

coup de grâce: 'Having known Colonel Burns personally, I feel convinced that if he had had the choice of the two galleries he would certainly have preferred to deposit his father's portrait among an assemblage of his distinguished fellow country-men, rather than in a mere collection of works of art (however excellent). The worthy Colonel cared nothing for art, but was devoted to his father's memory; and he did not leave the portrait to the National Gallery as a specimen of Nasmyth …'

Those who voted against the transfer, in addition to relying on the legal obstacle, referred to the fact that visitors, especially the many from abroad who came purely to see that particular painting, would be disappointed if it were 'removed from its accustomed place'. It was the National Gallery's only example of a portrait by Nasmyth (they already had a landscape, the kind of painting for which the artist was best known), and, besides, the Portrait Gallery had on loan the portrait of Burns by Peter Taylor. With hindsight they seem feeble arguments, but those against the transfer, who included Arthur Halkett (who was on the Portrait Gallery committee) and the sculptor John Steell, carried the day by ten votes to eight. The portrait would remain in the National Gallery for another thirty years.

The clearest impression of how the collection looked in its early days is given by the 1909 edition of the gallery's catalogue. The collection, exhibited entirely on the two upper floors, consisted of rather less than 700 items. All apparently had descriptive labels, though it is not clear if these went much beyond stating the identity of the subject and artist. Indeed, the discursive wall labels that museum and gallery visitors have become used to were not introduced in the Portrait Gallery until the early 1950s, and even later in the National Gallery. The catalogue, however, did provide quite extensive biographies of both sitter and artist. In addition to the paintings and sculptures, there was a plethora of other material, staggering in its variety and far beyond any notion of a 'pantheon'. In window cases were deeds, letters, autographs, the portrait medals mentioned above, and engraved portraits. Among them were a deed signed by Queen Elizabeth, original Burns manuscripts, two letters from Scott to his publisher John Ballantyne, and William Gladstone's copy of the Irish Home Rule Bill of 1893, with his autograph. This was linked to the portrait of Gladstone by Prince Troubetskoy that had been bought the previous year, and presumably the Scott letters were related to the little watercolour portrait of Ballantyne from the Watson Bequest of 1886. It all sounds vaguely chaotic, but in its multifarious way it is a forerunner of the far more coherent thematic displays using such material that would become popular in the second half of the twentieth century, particularly in the Portrait Gallery's series of historical loan exhibitions. The rooms on the top floor continued in this miscellaneous fashion, with a group of ninety-five drawings of Old Edinburgh by James Drummond and ninety-seven engraved portraits – mostly from the Watson Bequest. To cap this staggering variety, there was a selection of plaster busts from the Albacini collection – reproductions from the antique made by Carlo Albacini and bought by the Royal Institution in 1839. (Later consigned to a kind of storage purgatory, a number were rescued by Timothy Clifford in 1988 to decorate one of the staircases in the National Gallery.)

10 *Robert Burns* by Alexander Reid, 1795/6
W.F. Watson Bequest in 1886, PG 341

11 *Robert Burns* by Alexander Nasmyth, 1828
Bequeathed by Sir Hugh H. Campbell to the Scottish National
Gallery, 1894 and transferred to the Scottish National Portrait
Gallery, PG 1062

As already mentioned, in 1910 the Portrait Gallery's collection was augmented by twenty-five portraits from the Royal Scottish Academy, all ceded by the Academy as part of the arrangements that followed the creation of the National Galleries of Scotland in 1906. Among the portraits transferred at this time were the Raeburn full-length of John Wilson as a young man – that professor of moral philosophy who knew little of the subject, and, as the critic 'Christopher North', was to be one of the literary enemies of John Keats. (In 1984 he was joined in the collection by a beautiful pastel of his mother by Archibald Skirving, gifted by a direct descendant.) Most significant among the others were David Allan's stiff little portrait of James Craig, the planner of Edinburgh's New Town, a portrait of Allan himself painted in Rome by Domenico Corvi (the second major European painting to enter the collection) and the well-known pastel self-portrait by a pugnacious-looking Allan Ramsay [108]. This would be joined in 1929 by Ramsay's chalk drawing of his second wife, Margaret Lindsay, another gift from the former Secretary to the Board

of Trustees, Alexander Inglis. If there is any hint of a pattern in the portraits given by the Academy it perhaps lies in an emphasis on the history of the Academy itself – also included were a portrait of Lord Cockburn, who had played an important role in the award of their royal charter, and a self-portrait of its first president, George Watson.

Although there has been a growing tendency in recent times to see the collections of the three national galleries as one collection, particularly when there was a need to bolster the idea of a national collection of Scottish art, the Board of Trustees of the National Galleries of Scotland had initially emphasised that the collections of the Portrait Gallery and the National Gallery should be kept separate. At a meeting in July 1907 they had decreed that, while there could be 'free give-and-take … there should be no joint collection'. This meant that when works were transferred they were deleted from one register and added to the other. In the century that followed the initial transfer of 1889, quite a large number of items were moved from the collection of the National Gallery to the Portrait Gallery, and it is intriguing to see how the interests of a gallery devoted to the history of art gave way to those of a gallery devoted to the illustration of history – or, on occasion, did not give way. But, just as there seems not to have been any thought of transferring Raeburn's glamorous Mrs Scott Moncrieff, so there has never been any question that Raeburn's portrait of 'the skating minister', the Revd Robert Walker (a painting that has become by far the most famous of all Scottish portraits since its discovery in 1949) should hang in the National Gallery rather than the Portrait Gallery.

What would prove to be the most important group of works, both as portraits and as works of art, to migrate from the Mound to Queen Street during the twentieth century, were transferred in the period immediately following the First World War. Among them were the two major portraits of Burns by Alexander Nasmyth, the head and shoulders portrait of 1787 [101] and the posthumous small full-length, which shows Burns by the Old Brig at Alloway (bequeathed by Hugh Campbell) [111]. Until these transfers were made Burns had been represented only by the Miers silhouette, the miniature by Alexander Reid [110], the rather dubious portrait by Peter Taylor which was on loan, and the later copy by Skirving of the head and shoulders portrait by Nasmyth. It is curious that the three-fold historical resonance of Nasmyth's portrait had not been perceived earlier as something of exceptional relevance to the Portrait Gallery – Burns as a close friend of the artist, its link to the 1787 Edinburgh edition of the poems as the source for the engraved frontispiece and its long possession by the poet's son who had inherited it from his mother, Jean Armour.

Accompanying Ramsay's 1766 portrait of David Hume when it changed collections was William Dyce's full-length of a relatively unknown physician, James Hamilton, and Henri-Pierre Danloux's vast history painting depicting Admiral Duncan of Camperdown, which had recently been bequeathed to the National Gallery by the Earl of Camperdown [112]. The portrait of Hamilton, given to the National Gallery in 1870 by Heriot's Hospital, was large and in bad condition, and it is likely that it was being passed on because it had become an inconvenience. The

112 *Admiral Duncan* by Henri-Pierre Danloux, 1798

Bequeathed by the Earl of Camperdown to the Scottish National Gallery in 1919 and transferred to the Scottish National Portrait Gallery, PG 1065

portrait of Duncan was, of course, quite different – a dazzling piece of continental bravura depicting a great popular hero. Thereafter, a good deal of material was transferred in mostly haphazard fashion, the reasons being sometimes clear, at other times obscure or even questionable. For example, in 1950 a whole series of graphic items – portrait drawings of foreign or even unidentified subjects, often copies of copies – were transferred in what was little more than a weeding-out process by the newly founded Print Room in the National Gallery. With rather better reasons, most of the National Gallery's miniatures were transferred in 1980 and 1982. Though often of English or unidentified subjects, the miniaturists were mostly interesting Scottish artists, and this was the loosely formulated beginning of a development of the 1990s that saw the Portrait Gallery become home to a national and international miniature collection. With the addition of important collections on long-term loan, it became an undoubted centre of excellence in this field – although a field far from the gallery's original aims.

Sculpture had loomed large in the minds of those who had created the Portrait Gallery – portrait sculpture in Britain has been a quintessentially Victorian form – and this was expressed most emphatically on the exterior of the building. Inside the building, no visitor in the earliest years could have failed to be impressed by the great statue of Robert Burns by John Flaxman in the central hall, placed on loan (as it still is) by the City of Edinburgh who had had to remove it in 1863 from the Burns Memorial in Regent Terrace to prevent its deterioration in Edinburgh's sooty atmosphere. Among the earliest purchases in 1887 had been a group of original plaster models bought directly from the sculptor John Steell, who was unparalleled at portraying the established society of later nineteenth-century Scotland. A number of major pieces of sculpture would be among the other significant works that would follow the familiar route from the Mound to Queen Street between the 1920s and the 1960s when, apart from the minor works and the miniatures, the procedure ceased. Among these, both in 1924, were Patric Park's marble bust of David Octavius Hill (whose importance in the history of world photography was beginning to be appreciated) and Steell's bust of the Duke of Wellington of 1845 (made in preparation for the Wellington equestrian statue in front of Register House). Ten years later, and following no evident pattern, two other marble busts were transferred. These were Francis Chantrey's portrait of the political economist Francis Horner and Samuel Joseph's bust of David Wilkie. The bust of Horner had just been received by the National Gallery in bequest from Lady Murray and was transferred almost immediately. It may be that the Wilkie accompanied it as a way of enhancing the quality of the Portrait Gallery's collection of sculpture. Certainly, that quality was

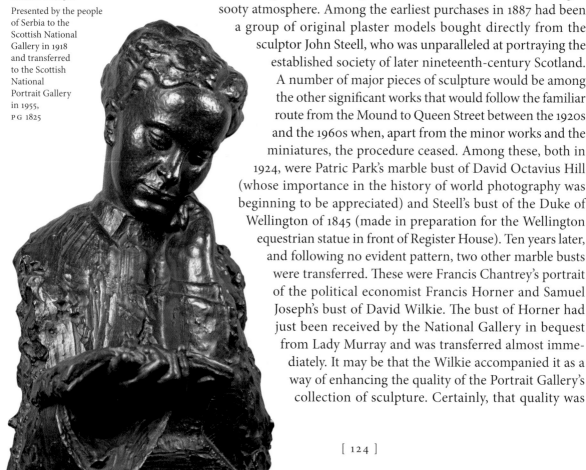

113 *Dr Elsie Maud Inglis* by Ivan Meštrović, 1918

Presented by the people of Serbia to the Scottish National Gallery in 1918 and transferred to the Scottish National Portrait Gallery in 1955, PG 1825

remarkably strengthened in 1955 by the relocation of the bronze memorial portrait of Elsie Inglis by Ivan Meštrović [113]. This touching portrayal of the surgeon who had virtually given her life in the service of Serbia during the First World War had been given by the people of that country to the Scottish National Gallery in 1918 in recognition of her sacrifice. In addition to its easily appreciated elegiac function, it must at the time have stood out as a work of emphatically modern art.

The aims of the fledgling Portrait Gallery, which had relied so much on private beneficence since its beginning, were given a boost in 1903 when government provided a purchase grant of £200. Not entirely niggardly at the time – and any annual residue was allowed to be carried over from year to year – that remained the figure until the Second World War when the trustees patriotically agreed to see it cut to £60. In the years following the war, the grant did rise substantially (as did inflation) so that by 1987 it stood at £110,000 – by this time, however, this constituted a proportion of a global sum granted to the National Galleries of Scotland and allocated to the three component galleries by the Director on a perceived basis of need. Thereafter, there was no specific allocation and a claim had to be established on a central fund which stood at about £1.1 million per annum.

While the early purchase grant could cope with the £15 required to buy works like William Nicholson's portrait of Scott's friend, Adam Fergusson, it is difficult not to compare the sum of £200 with the money that Findlay had made available. It has to be assumed that those in government who were able to imagine how the collection must grow believed that it would do so on the basis of gifts. This did happen, but as British art became more and more attractive to American collectors, prices rose rapidly and the problems of acquisition in the market had to rely more and more on trust funds held by the National Galleries and on special government grants.

This type of problem is illustrated by the purchase in 1935 (a time of dire economic difficulties) of one of the Portrait Gallery's best-known portraits, Raeburn's apotheosis of Sir Walter Scott – one of Raeburn's last portraits and evocative of the meeting in the light-swept studio in Edinburgh's York Place of Scotland's greatest writer, and its greatest painter [114]. It is also a case history of the problems of juggling and raising funds which more and more became the lot of curators. The painting had remained with the artist's family until 1877, when it had been sold by Christie's auction house. It then passed through a number of private collections (including that of the sugar magnate James Duncan of Benmore) before being bought in 1922 by the American collector Horace Harding for £12,000. James Caw had hoped to buy the portrait for the National Galleries, but had failed to raise sufficient funds, despite the interest of the future prime minister, Ramsay Macdonald, who had hinted that a friend might put up £10,000 towards its purchase. After the event, Caw wrote to Macdonald in a tone that has a hint of recrimination: 'I feel very disgraced as every Scotsman ought to feel that the Raeburn Scott has been allowed to go into exile.' In 1935, however, as the world economy crashed, the portrait reappeared on the market, this time with the art dealer, Knoedler & Company in London. Stanley Cursiter was now Director and determined to

114 *Sir Walter Scott*
by Sir Henry Raeburn,
1822

Bought with the
assistance of the Art Fund
in 1935, PG 1286

get the picture. His first port of call was John Jeffrey at Scottish Office, to whom he made three points: values had dropped and the picture could now be got for £10,000; the Galleries had been willing to pay £15,000 in 1922; and, 'in confidence', the dealer Joseph Duveen had offered the whisky company Dewar's £75,000 for Raeburn's Highland chieftain, the MacNab. The Scott would be a bargain. Six weeks later, Jeffrey informed Cursiter that special exchequer assistance had been refused. Cursiter had already written to Knoedler to say that he was determined that 'Sir Walter will remain on his native heath, even if we are bankrupt and with our credit exhausted.' Just short of bankruptcy, Cursiter was at length able to put together a sum of £9,622, and with a donation of £500 from the National Art Collections Fund was able to complete the purchase. Ever febrile, Cursiter could not resist writing to a secretary at Scottish Office, referring to Ramsay MacDonald's unfulfilled offer in 1922: 'I only trust he [the Prime Minister] is correspondingly elated that the picture has now returned.' Still elated himself, Cursiter then proceeded to upset the Secretary of the National Art Collections Fund by 'wondering whether a 5% contribution entitles you to a tablet on the picture!' The Secretary wrote back the following day asking if his reference to 5% was meant to be a joke, for if it was, 'the Chairman [Robert Witt] would be very distressed'. Cursiter, realising he had overstepped the limits of good taste, launched into a long and muddled apology: 'I am so sorry you ever dreamed for a moment that my 5% gibe was serious. I am afraid I have an incurably facetious nature … Metaphorically I have my hair in curl papers – we expect the Princess at any moment!' He meant, in fact, the Duchess of Kent, who, with the Duke, visited the National Gallery on 25 May when they were welcomed by the trustee D.Y. Cameron – who also happened to be Vice-Chairman of the National Art Collections Fund.

An early concern of the Gallery had been 'Portraits which would not likely be available for purchase', and Caw prepared a list of these in 1910 so that they could at least be photographed. This may have stemmed from the flood of great British portraits (of which Raeburn's Scott had been one) to wealthy collectors in the United States in the late nineteenth and early twentieth centuries at prices that seemed to put them beyond the reach of public collections, and which led to the founding of the National Art Collections Fund in 1903. The years of economic depression on both sides of the Atlantic that followed the First World War had stopped this flow, however, and some kind of stability was restored, before the impoverished state of Europe after the Second World War once again put the great family collections in Scotland, and elsewhere in Britain, at risk. The beginnings of this trend are illustrated by the acquisition in 1953 of one of the Portrait Gallery's most enduring masterpieces, Gainsborough's full-length portrait of John Campbell, 4th Duke of Argyll, from the Duke of Argyll of the day (the much-married and divorced 11th Duke) [116]. It is arguable that the painting is one of Gainsborough's greatest, his delicious brushwork creating a profoundly touching image of an elderly man, whose finery as a Scottish member of the Lords does not hide his impending mortality. The purchase came at the same time as the Portrait Gallery's annual purchase grant was raised from £200 to £250 – a glimmer of the end of post-war austerity. This pinpoints the long-standing imbalance between the funds provided for purchases and the cost of great paintings, for the price was £3,000 (although negotiations had started at £6,000). When it is recalled, however, that Raeburn's portrait of Scott had cost £10,000 nearly twenty years before when the market was depressed, it is clear that the price boom that would increasingly attract an aristocracy less prosperous than it had been had not yet taken place. It was a sale at what would come to seem a very modest price, a fact that would always rankle with the 11th Duke's successor.

As this new wave of selling increased, and while it was still possible to compete in the market without too much strain, the National Galleries were greatly enriched. As prices in recent decades have escalated to unimagined heights without any

115 *James Hamilton* *1st Duke of Hamilt*
by Daniel Mytens,

Bought with the assistance of the Art Fund, the National Heritage Memorial F and the Pilgrim Trust 1987, PG 2722

116 *John Campbell* *4th Duke of Argyll*
Thomas Gainsborc 1767

Bought in 1953, PG 15

concomitant increase in purchase funds, the flow of portraits from historical family collections has posed enormous financial problems. This has meant a constant reliance on bodies like the Art Fund (formerly the National Art Collections Fund) and the National Heritage Memorial Fund, the Heritage Lottery Fund, private fund-raising, special one-off government grants (which continue under devolution) and inheritance tax arrangements.

Another private collection like the Argyll one that would relinquish astonishing riches, this time over an extended period, was that of the dukes of Hamilton. This was a collection that had already been depleted by a sale in 1882, and another in 1919 when Hamilton Palace faced demolition. In 1987 the Portrait Gallery was offered the opportunity to purchase a full-length portrait by Van Dyck of the Carolingian statesman, the 1st Duke of Hamilton. However, the Hamilton collection contained another full-length portrait of the same man painted by Daniel Mytens in 1629 which, to those who were not hidebound by the canon of British art, seemed a far greater painting. It was a deeply perceptive portrait of the youthful courtier (who would be executed twenty years later, shortly after the king), and a work of colouristic brilliance [115]. This masterpiece had been briefly on loan to the Portrait Gallery early in the century and later hung in the Hamilton apartments in the Palace of Holyroodhouse. It had then been placed on loan in the National Gallery in the 1950s where it became famous as 'the man in the silver suit', and came to be seen as one of the stars of that collection. In 1973 it had been returned to the Palace of Holyroodhouse and to a degree forgotten.

In the event, and before relative values were explored, the Mytens was preferred to the Van Dyck and purchased as part of a package which included a startlingly different painting, Oskar Kokoschka's double portrait of Douglas, 14th Duke of Hamilton, aviator and amateur boxer, and his wife Elizabeth Percy. This latter portrait had been painted by Kokoschka during a prolonged stay at Lennoxlove in 1969 – when he is said to have greatly enjoyed copious amounts of Scotland's national drink. Valued at £380,000 and £60,00 respectively (prices that seem rational when compared to the inflated prices of today), the combined total of £440,000 was accumulated with grants of £260,000 from the National Heritage Memorial Fund, £70,000 from the National Art Collections Fund and £10,000 from the Pilgrim Trust. These sums were in addition to the £100,000 that the Portrait Gallery was able to draw from the central purchase fund of the National Galleries. This was a pattern of funding expensive purchases that would become typical.

As the Hamilton purchases were concluded, attention was turned almost immediately to the possibility of acquiring another remarkable modern painting, a portrait of the writer Naomi Mitchison by Wyndham Lewis [117]. The sitter had paid a visit to the Gallery and had toyed with the idea of giving or bequeathing the portrait. This raised great expectations which were never quite realised and it was not until 2003 that the portrait was acquired as a purchase for £100,000. Help on this occasion was provided by the Art Fund and the National Galleries' own Patrons organisation. It is a portrait of bright intelligence in every respect. Sickert had once called Lewis 'the greatest portraitist of this or any other time',

117 *Naomi Mitchison, Lady Mitchison* by Wyndham Lewis, 1938
Bought with the assistance of the Patrons of the National Galleries of Scotland and the Art Fund in 2003, P G 3351

an overstatement perhaps, but a remark that is reflected in the quality of this exceptional work.

Also close on the heels of the Hamilton pictures came negotiations to purchase another outstanding portrait from a private collection, Allan Ramsay's three-quarter length of his friend Hew Dalrymple, Lord Drummore, painted for the Edinburgh Musical Society in 1754 – at a cost of £25 [118]. The portrait had reached the marketplace by 1903 when it was bought at auction by the Broun Lindsay family for the remarkably low price of 13 guineas (£13.13s.). Its value to the Portrait Gallery lay in both its historical echoes and its sheer quality. The simple gravity of Drummore is realised by the most delicate and precise means imaginable, the gentle light that washes the room where he sits becoming a virtual metaphor for the enlightenment values that the sitter, and artist, represented – in the same year in which it was painted Drummore, Ramsay, and their friends David Hume and Adam Smith had founded that famous Enlightenment club, the Select Society. Although the portrait's owners expressed a hope that 'our dear picture can stay in Scotland', the Tate Gallery and the London National Gallery had also been alerted – and the painting would have graced either collection. In the event, the purchase was finalised quite quickly at £350,000, the National Heritage Memorial Fund and the National Art Collections Fund once again providing massive help.

Having chosen to sit out the opportunity to add a portrait by Van Dyck to the collection (although he was already represented, at least hopefully, by portraits of the theologian and diplomat Alexander Henderson and a full-length of the Lord Privy Seal, the 2nd Earl of Dunfermline), a small double portrait of exceptional quality by this artist – whose name has become almost synonymous with seventeenth-century portraiture – was acquired in 1996. The painting is a study from life of the two youngest children of Charles I, Princesses Elizabeth and Anne, exquisite in its immediacy. Purchased for £2.2 million from the representatives of the British Rail Pension Fund (art as a mere investment) with the now almost standard help from charitable funds, it was for long the most expensive painting to be acquired by the Portrait Gallery.

That accolade, however, if it is one, passed in 2002 to Charles Lees's vast 'action' portrait called *The Golfers*. Depicting a crucial stage in a golfing foursome played on the links at St Andrews in 1841, the players are intently watched by forty-eight famous, and less than famous, spectators. Lees painted the picture in 1847 for the engraver Alexander Hill and made use of the new art of photography to depict the subjects, a very early use of a technique that artists have used in various ways since. The painting was eventually acquired by the Cheape of Strathtyrum family and was bought from them for £2.5 million – with, appropriately, in addition to the usual donors, a contribution from the Royal and Ancient Golf Club.

The purchase of great paintings from the Hamilton collection did not quite finish with the acquisition of the Mytens and the Kokoschka in 1987. In 2002 another 'package deal' was concluded, with the purchase of two very different paintings for a combined price of £1.65 million. One of these was what could be regarded as a traditional Portrait Gallery acquisition, Gavin Hamilton's 'Grand

118 *Hew Dalrymple, Lord Drummore* by Allan Ramsay, 1754
Bought with the assistance of the National Heritage Memorial Fund and the Art Fund in 1989, PG 2800

Overleaf
119 *The Golfers* by Charles Lees, 1847
Bought with the assistance of the Heritage Lottery Fund, the Art Fund and the Royal and Ancient Golf Club in 2002, PG 3299

120 *Elizabeth Gunning, Duchess of Hamilton* by Gavin Hamilton, 1752/3

Bought with the assistance of the National Heritage Memorial Fund, the Art Fund and a contribution from the Wolfson Foundation in 2006, P G 3496

Tour' triple portrait of Douglas, the 8th Duke of Hamilton, his tutor Dr John Moore and his young son John. The other was a work that can be described as a contemporary history painting with a large topographical-cum-theatrical element. It illustrates an event in later Jacobite history, a celebration led by Prince James (the Old Pretender) of the elevation of his son Prince Henry to the cardinalate in 1747 before an elaborate stage set attached to the front of the Palazzo Muti in Rome [120]. Scintillating in colour, the elaborately costumed figures who circulate in the Roman piazza certainly breathe a credible sense of time and place into an aspect of the ever-enticing national story of the Jacobites.

The avalanche of Hamilton pictures was completed in 2006 by one final exceptional portrait, again by Gavin Hamilton, this time in his truly neo-classical mode: a full-length portrait of the famous beauty Elizabeth Gunning, Duchess of Hamilton, with her slim and yearning hound in sumptuous greys [121]. It is a painting that can be seen to play that double role that portrait galleries love – a portrait of a distinctive, intriguing individual from society's past and also a painting of such

121 *James III Congratulating his Son, Henry Benedict, on the Occasion of his Elevation to Cardinal York, July 1747* by Paolo Monaldi, Pubalacci and 'Silvestri', 1747–8

Bought with the assistance of the Heritage Lottery Fund and the Art Fund in 2001, P G 3269

122 *John Ker, 3rd Duke of Roxburghe* by Pompeo Batoni, 1761

Allocated to the Scottish National Portrait Gallery by H M Government, P G 2940

123 *Sir Alexander Morison* by Richard Dadd, 1852

Bought with the assistance of the National Heritage Memorial Fund in 1984, P G 2623

aesthetic value as to be a marker in the history of art. When its cost of £603,000 is added to the other purchases from the Hamilton collection, it can be seen that over a period of less than twenty years a sum of £2,693,000 had been expended on the acquisition of five paintings from one of Scotland's great ancestral collections.

Portraits from these long-established collections often carried an inducement to sell to a national collection in the form of certain tax advantages. An even greater advantage accrued in the form of portraits accepted by the Treasury in settlement of tax liabilities and allocated to a gallery or museum where they were considered to be relevant. In this way, over the past few decades the Portrait Gallery has been enriched by a number of works of outstanding quality that the early curators might have considered beyond their reach. These have included one of Angelica Kauffman's most vital female portraits, that of Jane, Duchess of Gordon, who was famous for riding a pig bareback through the streets of Edinburgh and offering a recruiting shilling from between her lips (amongst other distinctions); another female portrait by the German/Dutch painter Gerard Soest of the demure lutenist Lady Margaret Hay, Countess of Roxburghe, which is extraordinary for its flashing planarities of form; and Francis Grant's *A Meeting of the Fife Hounds* – a group portrait of hounds, horses and unabashed mankind in a recognisably Scottish landscape.

In a variation of this fiscal practice, the Portrait Gallery has benefited more obliquely – perhaps more directly in the long term – by being assigned ownership of portraits acquired by the Treasury providing they remain in situ – that is, in the historical (usually great house) context for which they were originally created. In some ways it is a curious arrangement for, although the Portrait Gallery is tasked with the care and preservation of the works, the gallery visitor gets no immediate benefit. Although meant to be accessible for viewing where they have been retained, a fee often has to be paid for entry to the house in question, which flies in the face of the proud principle of free entry to British galleries. The system, however, has the merit of keeping the work in the country. Portraits quietly acquired in this way include the lavishly robed peer, the great bibliophile John Kerr, 3rd Duke of Roxburghe by Pompeo Batoni, at Floors Castle [122], and a group of nine Campbell portraits by British artists of the first order (Cotes, Beechey and Lawrence) at Cawdor Castle.

This need by many of the older collections to take their great works of art to the market – which both challenged the fund-raising ability of the Portrait Gallery as well as enriching its collection – affected institutions as well as the aristocracy. An example is the strange and unsettling portrait of Alexander Morison, a pioneer in treating mental illness, by his patient Richard Dadd [123]. This painting was so little regarded by its owners, the Royal College of Physicians of Edinburgh, that its existence was virtually unknown. On the picture's rediscovery in 1979 it was placed on loan. Five years later it came to be seen as a way of part-funding a new lecture theatre the College was building, and it was placed on the open market with Agnew's of London. A sale was sought by a highly unusual method: closed bids were to be received by a fixed date. This was beyond the Gallery's normal method of purchasing at a fixed price or at auction (nearly always carried out free of charge on its behalf by another well-known dealer, Hugh Leggatt). Left quite in the dark to grapple with the imponderables of valuation (far from being any kind of science), the Gallery was unable to garner help from the National Art Collections Fund who thoroughly disapproved of this method of selling. A contribution, however, was offered by the National Heritage Memorial Fund and a bid was placed at £175,000. This, in the event, proved successful. It was a method of selling which, at least in the Portrait Gallery's experience, has fortunately not been repeated.

The rate at which the collection has expanded since its hesitant beginnings can be gauged by looking at the statistics of what can be termed the 'primary collection' – those works in the more or less traditional forms other than photography and leaving aside loans. The minimally illustrated catalogue of the collection published in 1951 listed 1,557 items, while the catalogue of 1977 contained 2,364 portraits. By the time of the production of the 1990 catalogue, which contained a large number of illustrations, the collection consisted of 2,780 works. In 2011, this number had risen to 3,675. These figures show an increasing rate of growth from about twenty-five works a year in the first sixty years of the Gallery's history to thirty-two a year shortly after its centenary in 1989. In the past two decades, however, this yearly acquisition rate has increased quite dramatically to some forty-two works. These latest figures can only be an indication of the widening of the gallery's perception of what visual material of a biographical/historical nature is relevant to the didactic purpose of a portrait gallery; a loosening of the strictures – even in some cases taboos – that bound the early curators. After the initial, rather ill-assorted, nature of the original displays there was a tendency to apply narrower criteria to what was relevant, typified by the protracted, intermittent discussion of admitting portraits of the living. There was no doubt also a long memory of the Carlylean view that portrait galleries were about heroes, a view that would never have countenanced pictures like James Paterson's *Surrender of the German Fleet* [88] or any of the topographical landscapes that were eventually acquired. With a certain irony, the changing pattern can be illustrated by the iconography of Carlyle himself: having stated the opinion that recent historical figures need only be illustrated by one portrait, he himself would come to be represented by more than half a dozen major images, ranging from John Linnell's portrait of the still-beardless young historian to Helen Allingham's intimate watercolour of the elderly sage in his study [124], or the great sedentary statue by Edgar Boehm carved in 1881, the year of Carlyle's death. It is also doubtful if he or the early curators could have accorded the equality in the hierarchy of genres that is enjoyed by photography – but a man of Caw's vision might just be imagined saying, 'you cannot have good portraits without good photographs'. Nor would the flippancy shown by the cartoonist H.M. Bateman in his drawing of Harry Lauder have been easily digested.

This opening up of parameters has quickened in recent decades. Notions of what

124 *Thomas Carlyle*
by Helen Allingham,
1879
Bought in 1915, P G 845

'from the life' means and how societal significance is measured have all been relaxed – nor do you have to be 'very Scottish' to be admitted. The 'pantheon' has gone, or been encompassed in something bigger. Yet, curiously, this new multifariousness of imagery echoes some of the earlier stages of compiling portrait collections. The idea of collective portrayal persists, like the old theme of *uomini famosi* – famous men, and women – a coming full circle as it were, where a group of portraits have a meaning for society beyond the individual, and indeed represent that society. Hence, the acquisition (a gift from an entity called New Edinburgh Ltd) of twelve bronze busts of modern Scottish poets ranging from Hugh MacDiarmid to Jackie Kay, some of them from life but the majority re-imaginings after the death of the subject. From life, by the very nature of the medium, are a number of series of photographic portraits: thirty contemporary Scottish actors – Peter Capaldi [125], Ewan McGregor, Robert Carlyle, Tilda Swinton – nearly all of them made in 2000; a group of twenty-six theatrical portraits by Richard Campbell that portray life in the Glasgow Citizens' Theatre from every conceivable angle – and reprise Adrian Wisniewski's painted group portrait of the three principal directors of the time (commissioned by the Portrait Gallery in 1994); as well as eighteen photographs by Luke Watson of religious figures representing many of the faiths now held in

125 *Peter Capaldi*
by Donald Maclellan,
1999
Bought in 2002,
PGP 284.16

126 *Kenny Dalgleish*
by Mark I'Anson,
2003
Commissioned by
the Scottish National
Portrait Gallery in 2003,
PG 3347

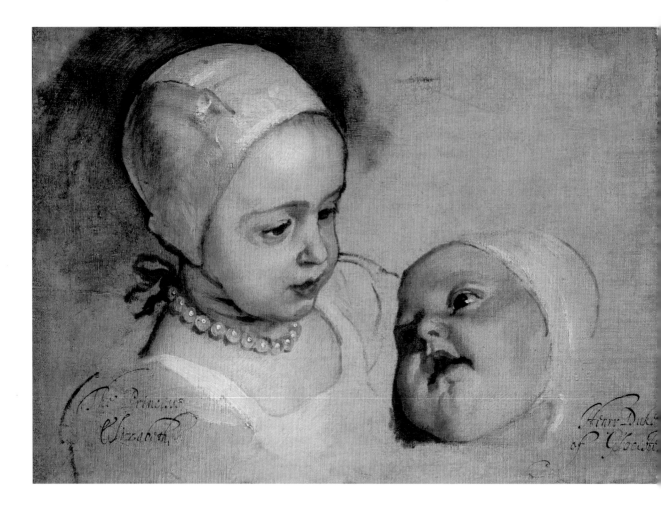

127 *Princess Elizabeth*
(1635–1650) and
Princess Anne
(1637–1640)
by Sir Anthony
van Dyck, 1637
Bought with the
assistance of the
Heritage Lottery Fund,
the Scottish Office and
the Art Fund in 1996,
P G 3010

128 *Mrs Agnes
Maclehose ('Clarinda')*
by John Miers, 1788
Presented by W.G.
Campbell in 1897, P G 567

Scotland. In each group there is a meaning bigger than the individual. In the same vein, a group of eleven Scottish footballers commissioned from Mark I'Anson in 2003 depicts the ideal soccer team from the post-war period [126]. Part of the rage that society now has for making lists (though Lord Buchan had made them more than 200 years earlier) and creating league tables of 'the best' or 'the greatest', such a series seems to mix the notions of 'the illustrious' with celebrity, a twenty-first century mode of connecting with the lives of others – others usually out of normal reach. Inevitably created from existing images rather than from life, they nonetheless represent society at a particular time – perhaps a time when values are uncertain and when the need for them is not satisfied by the old hierarchies.

It is all part of the yearning to connect that lies at the root of portrait galleries, and which they can satisfy in something like the way that Carlyle sensed – beyond aesthetics, but the connection established in the profoundest way within an aesthetic dimension that is not easily defined. Take two images from the collection, one from the earliest days, one from the recent past: the little ink silhouette on plaster of Agnes Maclehose by John Miers [128] and Van Dyck's study of Charles I's

little daughters, Elizabeth and Anne [127]. The first is entirely modest, though in
the diaphanous headdress, Miers creates a sense of space and movement beyond
mere silhouette that recreates that aura of sensuality that so entranced Robert
Burns. Whatever its limitations, the image was made from her cast shadow, so we
are in her presence. We know also that it must have been handled by Burns. That is
part of its unique meaning. The painting by Van Dyck is a purely painterly search
for the essential in the coming life of two little girls. Every mark is a true record
of what they were. Both the Miers and the Van Dyck in their different ways have
that almost limitless freshness, that breathless moment of briefly connecting with
a distant past that had seemed beyond reach.

CHAPTER EIGHT

THE NEXT CHAPTER

JAMES HOLLOWAY

O N 9 May 1994 the Secretary of State for Scotland, Ian Lang, issued a press statement in which he 'noted and welcomed' the trustees announcement that they had revised their initial intention in relation to the Scottish National Portrait Gallery. 'I am also prepared,' he continued, 'to give high priority to the refurbishment of that part of the Findlay building to be vacated by the National Museums of Scotland, to enable the trustees to display more of the National Galleries' Scottish collections on a permanent basis. I have invited the trustees to come forward in due course with costed proposals for this, which I will consider.'

Within a week the National Galleries of Scotland had issued its own press release in which a relieved and optimistic Keeper of the Portrait Gallery, Duncan Thomson, declared that

> ... the integrity of the Scottish National Portrait Gallery has been assured. In 1998 the Museum of Antiquities will relocate to the new Museum of Scotland in Chambers Street. By the year 2000 the Scottish National Portrait Gallery will have developed this additional space to continue to expand and develop. By being able to show works which are currently held in storage the Scottish National Portrait Gallery will meet the ever evolving needs of holding this important and historical collection in trust for the nation.

Duncan Thomson's vision of a new Scottish National Portrait Gallery was upbeat – rightly so, considering the challenges of the recent past. However, his date of the year 2000 for the completion of the project was premature, for it took a further seventeen years before the Museum of Antiquities' collections were removed, the two halves of the building reunited and the ambitious *Portrait of the Nation* project completed. By the opening date, the cast of all those most intimately concerned with the fate of the Portrait Gallery in the early 1990s – trustees, Director-General, Keeper, Secretary of State – had left the stage.

The project to refurbish the Portrait Gallery had always had two main aims. The first was the thorough renovation of the whole building that Robert Rowand Anderson had designed for John Ritchie Finlay in the 1880s. The second was the reinvigoration of a venerable but neglected institution by the imaginative deployment of its remarkable collection. *Portrait of the Nation* became the project title, and Page\Park of Glasgow was the architectural firm selected to realise the first of these aims. Their brief was to maximise display space whilst introducing those modern services that had hitherto been lacking. Rowand Anderson's architecture would be respected, but modern interventions would be contemporary in style and clearly differentiated. Their work has allowed the public once more to understand

129 Gallery 7, the Monument Gallery with Sir David Wilkie's *Self-portrait* and *Pitlessie Fair* on the left-hand wall, alongside *Sir Walter Scott* by Sir Henry Raeburn. Sir John Watson Gordon's portrait of James Hogg is on the free-standing screen

Reformation to Revolution

THE 'GLORIOUS REVOLUTION'

130 Views of the top floor galleries being hung in preparation
for the re-opening of the Gallery.

left, top and bottom: Gallery 1, Reformation to Revolution

above: Gallery 4, Imagining Power: The Visual Culture of the
Jacobite Cause

the logic of Rowand Anderson's simple but elegant plan and relish those details that had long been hidden. Nowhere has this been more rewarding than in the Square Room on the top floor, also known as the Raeburn Room. There, Rowand Anderson's elegant sandstone arcade was revealed after half a century hidden behind a partition wall [131]. Similarly, the 1930s ceilings in the two adjacent rooms were replaced with the original coving and top lighting. The library of the Society of Antiquaries of Scotland, designed by Rowand Anderson and fitted by Robert and Andrew Shillinglaw, was taken down and re-erected on the middle floor [132]. Page\Park were also able to fulfil one of Rowand Anderson's original intentions by converting the two smaller rooms at the east and west ends of the building from offices into galleries [137, 138]. The effect on the top floor has been dramatic: the re-creation of one of the most handsome suites of galleries in Britain, now dedicated to telling the story of Scotland from the Reformation to the end of the Victorian era [130].

One of the criticisms of the old building was that it was gloomy. The removal of the screens on the middle and ground floors, revealing Rowand Anderson's glazed arcades, has lightened up these great spaces and accentuated the contrast

131 Gallery 6, Blazing with Crimson: Tartan Portraits

between them and the double-height Great Hall, untouched save for cleaning and improved lighting. New vistas on the ground and top floors have been created, allowing the building to be read and navigated with ease. Great care was taken to re-use wherever possible the original furniture, display cases, and even radiators. The original parquet floors, pine to the east and ash to the west, were restored. But new features such as the large glass lift and a bold mezzanine floor providing staff accommodation are uncompromisingly of the early twenty-first century: clean, functional and distinct. The total effect is a tribute to the genius of Rowand Anderson, successfully adapted to the demands of the public in a modern gallery.

For the first time in its history the Portrait Gallery is able to provide facilities for educational classes [135]. Tucked under the eastern mezzanine is a glass-fronted studio, alongside a small lecture theatre and a room available for children to use for meals. At the centre, there is a space where project work can be exhibited, and the National Galleries of Scotland's Education Department is accommodated nearby. This commitment to education is at the heart of *Portrait of the Nation* and the choice of exhibitions presented is related closely to Scotland's national curriculum.

132 The Society of Antiquaries Library reinstated in the west side of the building

Clockwise from top left:

133 Part of the area devoted to the Education Department with views to the Contemporary Gallery on the ground floor

134 The walkway at mezzanine level through to the curatorial offices

135 The Contemporary Gallery and the education activity room

136 View from the curatorial offices looking down to the ground floor and the area for the new shop

Out of the Shadow:
Women of the Nineteenth Century

137 Gallery 9, one of the new galleries converted from what was originally office space

A curator is linked to a member of the Education Department in scoping and preparing their exhibitions.

Also new, indeed the first in any public gallery in the country, is a dedicated area for photography exhibitions. The collection of photography is one of the greatest assets of the Portrait Gallery. Based on the foundation of the remarkable calotypes taken by David Octavius Hill and Robert Adamson in the 1840s, but embracing much more, it is of world importance. The status and expansion of the collection owes much to the scholarly work of Sara Stevenson who was the collection's curator for nearly forty years. During her tenure it was immeasurably enhanced by great gifts, especially those from the Riddell and Muir Wood families and from the Edinburgh Photographic Society. Additionally, the collection has benefited from many works generously presented by living photographers.

It is of course the collection of the Scottish National Portrait Gallery that is its chief resource and which will provide, over time, a succession of exhibitions, large and small, to illuminate Scotland's past and present. One of the frustrations of the old building was how little space there was for display. It had merely three galleries on the top floor (there are now nine), only the western half of the middle floor was accessible, and on the ground floor what spaces there were for display seemed haphazard and temporary – which indeed was the case. More space now enables the staff to present topics in depth, and the simplicity of Rowand Anderson's design allows an easy circuit through the building.

Early on in the project it was decided that the presentation of the collection should not be static but revolve. While the displays in the larger galleries might be expected to remain unaltered for several years those in the smaller galleries would change more often and be of a size to tour round the country. Portraits otherwise in near-permanent storage would have their moment on display in an appropriate context. As part of the National Galleries of Scotland, the Portrait Gallery is able to borrow works of art with ease from its sister galleries, the Scottish National Gallery and the Scottish National Gallery of Modern Art. David Wilkie's *Pitlessie Fair*, for instance, normally hangs at the Scottish National Gallery on the Mound as the artist's first undoubted masterpiece, and it is in the context of Wilkie's art in particular and Scottish art in general that it is shown. Displayed in the Portrait Gallery, Wilkie's painting subtly changes [129]. It becomes primarily a depiction of rural life in early nineteenth-century Fife – the visual equivalent of Sir John Sinclair's abstract of parish life, the *Statistical Account of Scotland* which Wilkie's father as minister responsible for Pitlessie must laboriously have completed. Conversely, portraits not needed for display in the Portrait Gallery will be made available to the other national galleries or indeed elsewhere.

Although portraiture hardly existed in Scotland before the middle of the sixteenth century, the nation's earlier history is represented through the decorative elements that enhance the building. The frieze, the murals and the sculptures on the façade take Scotland's history back to the Stone Age. This makes Scotland's Portrait Gallery unique amongst its peers. Of course, those portraits of St Columba, William Wallace or Macbeth are fanciful, but from the time of the Reformation vivid and authentic portrait painting flourished and dominated Scottish art [130]. Until well into the nineteenth century portraiture was Scotland's chief expression in the visual arts. The Portrait Gallery therefore both holds Scotland's collection of national portraits and contains the first chapters of the story of Scottish art. An acknowledgement of this dual role was taken in the early-1980s when the policy was adopted to acquire Scottish portraits of outstanding aesthetic interest whether or not the sitter was notable. The exhibitions reflect this commitment to Scottish art and the Portrait Gallery's role as custodian and advocate.

The separate exhibitions presented at the re-opening in December 2011 were conceived as part of an over-arching scheme of five key areas: Reformation, Enlightenment, Empire, Modernity and Contemporary. They chart a chronological route through Scotland's history and were chosen as periods when Scotland reacted most energetically with the wider world [139]. The historic resonances of the building itself and the fame of many of the great iconic portraits have led people to think of the Portrait Gallery as merely concerned with the past. As Duncan Thomson has already shown, however, portraits of contemporaries were accepted early on in the Gallery's existence. A special programme of commissioning portraits

138 Gallery 12, one of the new galleries converted from what was originally office space

139 Gallery 11, The Modern Scot, showing Alexander Moffat's painting *Poets' Pub*

of eminent contemporaries, which was introduced in 1982, reinforced this. The commissioning process continues and the most recent people to agree to sit for their portraits include multiple world and Olympic champion track cyclist Chris Hoy and the legendary championship golfer Colin Montgomerie. In its early days the Gallery's policy for acquisition and display followed Thomas Carlyle's belief in the power of heroes to inspire, and the resulting nineteenth-century notion of good citizenship and a belief in the power of good examples to promote emulation. In the millennium year of 2000 the Gallery chose to take stock of what those notions meant in Scotland at the start of a new century. It was agreed that great and inspiring lives could be encountered amongst much wider sections of society than Carlyle might have imagined, and the exhibitions mounted that year, *A Shepherd's Life*, *Health of the Nation* and *Men of the Clyde*, in particular, celebrated the heroic in 'ordinary' lives. Scotland is a small country which retains enduring values of clan and kinship. It seemed appropriate for its National Portrait Gallery to reflect that tight sense of national community. The programme has continued with exhibitions looking at the work of servants, (*Below Stairs*, 2004), the role of women (*Modern Women*, 2004/5) and the police (*Force*, 2007). Working alongside the Education Department, the Gallery has been connected with further community projects which have both involved and engaged audiences well beyond the Gallery's walls: with *Parallel Lives* (2002/3), Charles Lees's *The Golfers* [119] was introduced to a group of young people who would normally never visit the Gallery, and used to help them make parallels with their own lives. *Mirrors: Prison Portraits* (2010) involved offenders in five prisons developing self-portraits mediated by professional artists. *Silver City Soul* (2011) was a portrait of Aberdeen and its citizens, through their own eyes. Shortly after the Gallery shut for renovation in April 2009, but before the contractors moved in, a group of young graffiti artists were invited into the building to represent their own contemporary heroes and role models on the walls of the temporary exhibition space on the ground floor. The Gallery reopened briefly during the weeks of the Edinburgh Festival to show the project, which was entitled *Rough Cut Nation* [61].

The new Portrait Gallery will be a place where topics of national interest will be presented and debated. When the First Minister, Jack McConnell, condemned sectarianism in Scottish sport, the Gallery commissioned Mark I'Anson to create Scotland's ideal football team. Working with *The Herald* newspaper, eleven players and a manager were selected, drawn from across the sectarian divide to form *Scotland's Dream Team* [126]. The exhibition, which opened its cross-Scotland tour at Hampden Park in 2003, was shown in more venues across the country than any other exhibition ever mounted by the Portrait Gallery. Immigration and emigration have been twin features of Scottish life for centuries. The Scottish Diaspora numbers many millions, far greater than the number of Scots at home. Scotland's contribution to all parts of the globe will be celebrated in *Faces and Places*, the media project for the new Gallery. It will also be examined in the Migrations Stories Gallery [138] on the middle floor as will the contribution of new communities in Scotland. *A Scottish Family Portrait,* an exhibition of photographs of prominent

Pakistani Scots commissioned from Verena Jaekel, shown alongside a new film by Sana Bilgrami and a display on a Scots-born teacher in Lahore, was planned as the opening Migrations Stories exhibition.

Portrait of the Nation has involved staff working right across the National Galleries of Scotland for several years, with a huge amount of effort from a wide variety of skilled specialists. The sum of £17.6 million was needed to achieve the project. In November 2007 came the very welcome news that Scottish Government had pledged £5.1 million. A month later, the Portrait Gallery passed the stringent first stage of a Heritage Lottery Fund application. The confirmation of a grant from

140 The Society of Antiquaries' window

141 Mary Legget Bowman by Alison Kinnard for the new donor window

the Heritage Lottery Fund of £4.8 million came in April 2009, just days before the scheduled closure. An international fund-raising scheme was then started to raise the remaining £7.7 million. This was not an easy moment for the National Galleries of Scotland, with a commitment already in place to secure with Tate the quite exceptional collection of contemporary art, ARTIST ROOMS. At the same time, although not publicly announced, was the ambition to acquire those two supreme works by Titian, *Diana and Actaeon* and *Diana and Callisto* from the Bridgewater Collection. With another Director-General and a different body of trustees a quite understandable decision to postpone the Portrait Gallery project might well have been taken. Fortunately, the decision was taken that *Portrait of the Nation* must go ahead.

A number of imaginative schemes were thought up to encourage donations. *Put*

Yourself in the Picture allowed anyone to download a photograph of themselves, or someone they wished to remember, to appear on screen in the re-opened building. The stars on the ceiling of the Great Hall which, in the words of the artist William Hole, formed 'a zenith map of the northern sidereal hemisphere', were offered to potential benefactors. Figures from the frieze were also offered for adoption. The most generous donors could name a room, with the opportunity to be included on the specially commissioned donor window [141]. To commemorate the opening of the Museum of Antiquities on 13 August 1891, John Ritchie Findlay had commissioned a stained-glass window with the portraits of the office-bearers of the Society of Antiquaries of Scotland with their patron, Queen Victoria, who appeared at the top above the royal arms and the seal of the society [140]. The renowned glass artist, Alison Kinnaird, who had worked on the completion of the Marquess of Bute's decorative schemes at Mount Stuart, was commissioned to create a new donor window for the Portrait Gallery to be placed alongside the Antiquaries' window at the top of the eastern staircase. The portrait of Queen Elizabeth II will preside over symbols of the Scottish Government and Heritage Lottery Fund, our two principal donors. Below will be the garlanded and labelled portraits of the twenty-three most generous benefactors, with the allegorical figure of Winter and the re-opening date, the scheme thus mirroring the original window. Alison Kinnaird, working with Patrick Ross Smith, would provide the only new work of art to be commissioned for the Portrait Gallery which, despite the magnificent historical fanfare of the Great Hall, was always quite modestly ornamented. On the eve of the Scottish National Party's historic victory at the General Election of May 2011 a further Scottish Government grant of £2 million completed the capital fund-raising campaign, ensuring that the restoration of the Scottish National Portrait Gallery would be finished on time and on budget. At a critical moment in the country's history the future of Scotland's shrine to national identity – and inside it her unrivalled collection of historical and contemporary portraits – has been triumphantly secured.

Overleaf:

142 The renovated ground floor of the Gallery

BENEFACTORS

AS AT 23 OCTOBER 2011

THE · MONUMENT · TRUST

Major Donors

American Patrons
James and Morag Anderson
The Bacher Trust
The Barcapel Foundation
Ena Baxter Associates
The Binks Trust
Mary Legget Bowman
Ewan and Christine Brown's
 Charitable Trust
Ian Lyon Buchanan and Mary
 Sheila Irwin Buchanan
Richard and Catherine Burns
Colin Clark
Douglas and Marjorie Connell
Cordis Charitable Trust
Creative Scotland
The Drambuie Liqueur Company
Dunard Fund USA
Edinburgh Decorative and
 Fine Arts Society
Jo and Alison Elliot
John Ennis
The Faculty of Advocates
Esmée Fairbairn Foundation
James Ferguson
The Finnis Scott Foundation

The Hugh Fraser Foundation
Friends of the National
 Galleries of Scotland
The Gannochy Trust
Gavin and Kate Gemmell
G. C. Gibson Charitable Trust
Donald and Sally Hardie
James Holloway
The Hope Scott Trust
The Inches Carr Trust
Sir Brian and Lady Ivory
Sir Raymond and Lady Johnstone
Mrs Geraldine Kirkpatrick's
 Charitable Trust
Brian and Lesley Knox
Barrie and Janey Lambie
The Lord and Lady Leitch
Lindsay's Charitable Trust
Family Maccoll
Donald and Louise MacDonald
Lady Lucinda Mackay
The MacRobert Trust
Nancie Massey Charitable Trust
Alexander and Elizabeth McCall Smith
The Henry Moore Foundation
The Morton Charitable Trust
Allan and Carol Murray
Walter and Norma Nimmo
Patrons of the National
 Galleries of Scotland
Charles and Ruth Plowden
Miss M. B. Reekie's Charitable Trust
Mr and Mrs David Reid
The Robertson Trust
The Ross Girls
The Russell Trust
Alastair and Elizabeth Salvesen
Mel Seiden and Janine Luke
Gerald and Margo Smith
St Catherine Trust
Stevenston Charitable Trust
Ian and Flora Sword
William Syson
The Tam O' Shanter Trust
Ben and Lucy Thomson

The George and Margaret
 Trotter Charitable Trust
The Tulip Trust
Turcan Connell
Sarah Whitley and Graham Whyte
The Wolfson Foundation
WREN
Zachs-Adam Family

Donors

To celebrate the life of Euan
 Anderson Abel
Lord and Lady Abernethy
Elizabeth Adam of Blair Adam
Jim, Janet and Richard Adams
Mrs Judith Adams
R. Adams
Martin and Patricia Ahrens to
 celebrate the birth of Jack Ahrens
Mary R. Ainsworth
Air Power & Hydraulics Limited
Lady P.A. Airey
The Right Hon. the Countess of Airlie
 and the Right Hon. the Earl of Airlie
Ross Aitken
Pat Akhurst
Jane and Tony Aldgate
John Aldridge
Elizabeth Allan
Mr James Allan and Mr Christian Merlet
Margaret and Margaret Allan,
 for our own Glasgow Boys
Mrs Margaret Allen
Ken and Katie Allstaff, Aberfeldy
Elaine Anderson
Mrs M. Anderson
In celebration of the 90th birthday
 of Robert Rome Anderson
In memory of Ian Andrew
Patricia R. Andrew
Jo Anthony Boyce and Chris
 Anthony (donating a star for
 our mother, Nan Anthony)
Irené Archer
John and Jim Archer

Marjory Archibald

Mrs Jean A. Arkieson

Finlay Armstrong

Zoe Armstrong

Robin G. Arnott

Sheana and Victor Ashton

Graham Atherton and
    Claudine Rebersat

Sir Michael and Lady Atiyah

Mrs Valerie Atkinson

Meta Auld

David Austin, loving husband and dad

Isobel Baillie

Susanne Baird

Lady Balfour of Burleigh

Dr Jean Balfour

Christine Ball

Miss Ruby Jean Ball

Oliver and Victoria Barratt

For Simon, Ava and Oscar to
    celebrate the lives of Eileen,
    Peter and Margaret Barrett

David and Jane Barrie

The Misses Barrie Charitable Trust

Mrs Sue Barwell

Nick and Judith Bateman

Miss Isobel Baxter, Edinburgh

Patsy Baxter

Robert A. Bayliss

Mrs Sheila Bealey

Mr Colin Beattie

Mary Rose Beaumont

Mr and Mrs S. and A .Beck

For my beloved grandaughter
    Daisy Renée Beeson

To celebrate the life of James Wylie Begg

The Bell Family, Dunfermline

Sherrif A.M. Bell

Charles Edward Sinclair Bell 1965–1969

Graham and Marion Bell

Halla Beloff

Dr Claire Benton

William and Elizabeth Berry

Diana Bertoldi

B. Berwick on celebrating
    our 45th Anniversary

Jane M. Bett

In memory of J. Kenneth Billman,
    a Scot displaced to America

David and Alison Binnie

Ailsa and Colin Bird, in
    memory of Sarah Bird

In memory of Mary Bird (née
    Greer), mother of Ruth,
    Freda, Susan and Stanley

Mr and Mrs Henry J. Black

Doreen and Robert Black

Miss Shona Black

Trudy Blaikie

Roger and Diana Bland

Miss L.M. Blount

Dr and Mrs Tony Blythe

To celebrate the birth of James
    Alexander Boag-Thomson
    on 27 January 2011

J.L. Boase

The Boissiere Family, Edinburgh

E Michael Bottomley

Bourne Fine Art

In memory of Mary Legget Bowman

To commemorate the happy marriage
    of Margaret and Arthur Bowring
    of Newport on Tay, 1953–2007

Bette and David Boyd,
    diamond wedding 2012

Jane Boyd

Mr and Mrs David Bradley

Miss Inez Brady

Mr Roy Brady

Judith M. Brearley

Ellen Breheny

For Drew Bremner, Vicki Brown and
    their descendants, from Pepy (1967)

David John Brewer

Mrs Barbara Brocklehurst

Louise Brodie

To celebrate the 60th birthday
    of Philip Hope Brodie

David and Janey Brogan

Julia, Rory, Catherine and
    Donald Brown

Iain Gordon Brown

Irene J. Brown

Miss Isobel Brown

Kevin R. Brown

Lyn Brown in memory of
    Margaret Thorburn

Pauline E. Brown

Philip Brown

Miss Alicia Bruce

David Bruce

Eleanor Bruce

The Hon. James Bruce

Lady Bruntisfield

May Brunton

Dr Joycelyn Bryce

In memory of Ian Buchanan

Mr and Mrs Nigel Buchanan

Catherine I. Buick

Annette Bull

Jeremy M. Burnet and family in
    memory of Jen Burnet

Alfred David Burnett

Catriona Burns on behalf of Alice
    Rose Burns, Hector James
    Burns and Isla Louise Burns

Isla Burns

Joanna Burns

In loving memory of Liz Burns

Remembering David Burnside, a much
    loved brother, from Janis and Graeme

James Burnside

George and E. Kay Burt

Sheila and Dick Burtles

Hilary Burwell

Mrs Sandra A. Burwell

John and Joan Busby, celebrating
    art and music

Thomas Bush

Dr Norman E. Butcher, geologist

Kathy Butcher

Jennifer Bute for John Bute

Vincent Butler's family

Lady Butter cvo

Jane Butters

Lady Jane Buxton

Halcyon Byers

To celebrate the birth of Catriona
    Irene Byrne on 13 August 2009

Dr Evelyn Byrne

To celebrate the birth of Ruairidh Gerald
    Provan Byrne on 29 July 2011

John and Anna Cahill

Ann and Alan Cairns, St Andrews

J. Graham Callander

Lady Mary Callander

Rhona Callander – a gift from
    friends for a special birthday

To Callum with love from Lynn

Mr and Mrs Selwyn Cambridge

Ms Elizabeth Cameron

George Cameron

Hazel Cameron

Ms Helen Cameron

Ken Cameron

Lord Cameron of Lochbroom

Roderick Cameron

Alasdair Campbell

Julia Campbell

The Carr Family

Mrs Sally Carr

Eve Carnson

Ian Carter and Sabine Klaus

Lady Carter

To celebrate my love for
    Matthew Cartmell

David and Anne Casson

Nicola Catterall

Mr Patrick Chaland

Mr Alan Chalmers

Alison Chalmers

Betty Chalmers

John and Gwyneth Chalmers

To celebrate the life of Samuel Chandley

Elizabeth Chapman

The Charitable Trust of 1965

The Chater Family

Michael and Jennifer Cheesbrough

In memory of Kate Chetwynd

Judith Chisholm 2010

To celebrate the life of John
    Duncan Christie

Mr C.E. Christison

Hazel Clancy

Alison Clark

The Revd Dr Ian D.L. Clark

Linda Clark

Michael and Deborah Clarke

Georgina Clayton

Ranee Cleland born 21 September
    1930 – happy 80th

Patricia A. Cochrane

The Vivienne and Sam Cohen
    Charitable Trust – in memory
    of Professor Sam Cohen

Esther Cohen

Anne Colclough

Mr Rod Cole

Joanna Cole-Hamilton

Sally Cole-Hamilton

Norma-Ann and Rob Coleman

Denise Colledge

Mr Stuart Collinson

Colonel and Mrs G.J.L. Coltart

Ivy Alice Colville, precious grandaughter

Sheila Colvin

Mr Joel Conn

Iain Connon

The Connor Family, Edinburgh

Charles L. Cook

Anna Cooper

The Corbett Family

Shona Corner

Joyce Cottle

Elizabeth Coull

Mrs Lucinda Coulthard

Robbie, Sara and Blair Couper
    to celebrate the life of their
    Dad Robert Couper

Herbert Coutts MBE, KM

C.H. Cowan

Mrs D.B. Cowan

Michael John Coward

Mr Alan Cowe

Remembering Bill Crabbie

To celebrate the life of Marguerite
    Crane, who loved this gallery
    and inspired a love of its works
    in others, from her children

Dorothea Crawford

Doris Crichton

Pat and Tom Crombie

Mrs S.M.J. Crosfield

Frances Crow

Norman Christon Crow 1925–2009

Cruden Foundation Limited

Dr and Mrs John Cruikshank

David and Maria Cumming

Pauline Cumming

Dr P. Cundill

Michael and Jocelyn Cunliffe

Jennifer Cunningham and John Rowland

John and Kay Dale

The Dalton Family

For Jane Darkes from
    Anandan Tanabalan

Mrs Vivienne Darvell

Jillian Davey

Professor Colin Davidson
    born 18 September 1934

Nicola and Duncan Davidson

Moria Davidson

Professor Peter Davidson

Mrs Yvonne Davidson

Colin Cameron Davies

Tom Davies

James Dawnay

Eric and Margaret Dawson

Diane Day

Christine De Luca

Robert and Ilona Delamere

Viv Delmonte

Mrs Elizabeth Dent

Karina Dent

Diana Dey

Susan Diamond

Fiona Dick

Robert Dick

Eluned Dickinson

Ann Dickson and family, to celebrate
    the life of Fiona Burns Dickson

Anne and Arthur Didcock

John and Audrey Dilks

Rebecca Dobash

Doreen Dodd

Ian and Barbara Doig

Anne Donaldson for the
    Donaldson Family

Anne and William Donnelly

Shona Dougall

Ms Cora Douglas

To celebrate the life of J. Loudon Downs

Jean D. Doyle

Kate Doyle

To celebrate the life of Kathleen Doyle

Barbara Drummond, the best
    mum in the galaxy, lots of
    love Jamie and Lorna

In grateful memory of our parents,
    Gordon and Doreen Drummond,
    who loved the Galleries of Edinburgh,
    Gordon, Andrew, and Ian Drummond

Jamie and Lorna Drummond

Alison Duff

To celebrate the 30th birthday
    of Lynne Duff

Ronald and Jane Duff

To celebrate the 80th and 75th birthdays
    of Ronald and Jane Duff from Tom
    and Natalie Duff and family

Mr Stanley H. Duffus

Mrs Ena M. Dunbar

To celebrate the life and work of Sir
    Robert Rowand Anderson, Architect
    of the Scottish National Portrait
    Gallery and Founder of The Royal
    Incorporation of Architects in
    Scotland – Sir James Dunbar-Nasmith

Ann Dunan for the Duncan Girls

C.B. Duncan

Mrs E. Duncan

William Watson Duncan

The Dunmore Family

Sir Simon Dunning

Miss Alice Dunphy

Moira Dunworth

Dr Martin Eastwood

James and Dana Edgar

Edinburgh Old Town Association

Eddie Edmonstone – a birthday
gift from Deborah Bennett

Elizabeth and David Edward

Mr George Edwards

Mrs Georgina Elliot

Jill P. Elliot

R. John Elliot

Andrew Elliott

Archie Elliott

To celebrate the 50th birthday
of Sandra Ellis

Mark Webster in celebration
of G.R. Elmsie

Dr Dave Evans

Linda and Ryan Evans

In celebration of Phyllis Evans and
Sam Evans by Rosie Sinden-Evans

F. Hugh Eveleigh

Elizabeth Farquhar

Greta Ferguson

Mrs Elizabeth Ferrard and
Mr David Ferrard

Aileen Ferrigan

Dr Angus Findlay

Ian Fingland

Martin Finlayson

To celebrate the life of Irving Finn

Mrs Cherry Fleming

J.E. Fleming

Tom Fleming CVO, OBE

Hilary Flenley

Andrew Fletcher

Chris and Claire Fletcher

Marion Flett

Freya, Paul and Karen Flockhart

To celebrate the work of the distinguished
German novelist Theodor
Fontane who loved Scotland

Graeme Forbes

To celebrate the life of Duncan
Hugh Fraser Forrest

In memory of R.S. Forrest from his
granddaughter Patricia Millar

Simon and Gemma Forrest

William Fortescue

Donald and Petrina Fortune

Carol Foster

Laurence and Helen Fowler

Ms Virginia Fowler

Mrs Jean Fowlie

Jillian Franklin

Alexander Fraser

Sir Charles Fraser

Colette Fraser

Mr Peter S. Fraser

Peter and Jane Freshwater

The Friends of Morita, The
Victor Murphy Trust

Mr John Gallacher

Gail Gardiner

Robert, Emma and Tommy Gargan,
grandchildren of Sir Robert Cowan

The Garrett-Cox Family

Q 61 go: Light is the hand that loves

Dr Henry H. Gebbie

Robert Gemmell, Troon

Mrs Patricia Gerard

To celebrate the life of Leslie Gerber

The Hilda and Johnny Gibb
Charitable Trust

Mrs Jennifer Gibb

Kathleen Gibb

Angus Gibson

Barbara Gillie

Dedicated to Ann Marie Gilmore

To celebrate the life of Professor Duncan
Munro Glen from his family

Eric Glendinning

Goethe-Institut

Mr David Goldie

Kay Ames Goodall

Sir Matthew and Lady Goodwin

C. Ralph Gordon

Margaret and Alan Gordon

To celebrate the life of Walter Gordon
of The Warehouse, Glasgow and The
Thrie Estaits Antiques, Edinburgh

Heather, Cara and Murray Gourdie

Norma Gourdie

John Cook and Caroline Gow to
celebrate their marriage

Marina Graham

Patricia Graham

Joy Graham-Marr

Fiona Grant Robertson

Sheena Grant

Miss Yvonne R.F. Grant

T.L. Graveson

Mrs Aileen Gray, Edinburgh

Mrs Aileen Gray, Stromness

Miss Ailsa Gray

Jim and Jennifer Gray

For Gregor and Finlay, the
stars in our firmament

Mrs Jane Griffiths

Mrs Elizabeth Guest

Gail Guest

Ivor Guild

Mrs I.A. Guthrie

In memory of James W. Guthrie
1906–1976, of Glasgow and North
Berwick: Eastern Banker and a
beloved husband and father, always
enraptured by the firmament

Mrs Mary Haggart

Martin and Petronella
Haldane of Gleneagles

Mrs Elspeth M. Hall

Mr Ian W. Hall

Isobel A. Hall

Beatrice Hamilton MacDonald

James Hamilton

From the Hamilton, Millar and Steedman
Families to celebrate the life of Professor
Patrick J.S. Hamilton FRCP, 1934–1988

In memory of Andy Hamnett

To celebrate the Lives of Jack
and Betty Hannah

Keith Hannay

Alexander Harper

Reverend and Mrs Harris

John Alexander Don Harrison

Gladys Hart

George and Jean Haskell

Mrs Eileen Havard-Williams

Mr and Mrs Michael Havinden

Mrs Anne Hawley-Groat

Mr and Mrs Alexander Hay

Cynthia Hay

Rita C. Hayes

Meg Heggie

From the loving family of Judy Heller de
Gonzalez to celebrate her 60th birthday

Mr James Helliwell

Jude Hemsley, Kinross

Alex Henderson

Carol and Shields Henderson

Miss E.C. Hendry's Charitable Trust

James S. Hendry

Ms Patricia Herd

Jeremy Hewer

Mrs Moira Heywood

Lucinda Higginson

Fiona Hill
Mr Ronald Hill
Frank Hitchman
Mrs Eleanor Hodges
G. Hodgson
Mrs Louise Hogg
Joan Hoggan
Sue Holder
Angela Holliday, West Linton
Dr Derrick Holliday, West Linton
Edward Holloway
For James Holloway from the
    Holloway / Briant Evans Family
Ms Kirsty Holmes
The Right Hon. Lord Hope
    of Craighead K T
In memory of Graham Frank Horsman
    (1951–2010), donated by his family
Mrs P.M. Housley
Mrs Moira Houston
To celebrate the life of John V. Howard
Dr Peter Howell and Dr Janet Howell
Mr Ian Howie
Mrs Elizabeth N. Howitt
Kathleen Hughes
Dr David Hughson and Odile Hughson
Kathleen and John Hull
Ian and Ann Hume
Rosy Hume and Rhona Shepherd
In memory of Mary Katherine Humfrey
Fatima Huq
Sue E. Hussin
Diana Hutchings
Safeena Andrea Theresa Hutchison
To celebrate the life of David
    Hutton 1955–2009
Dale Idiens, in memory of 'The
    Beautiful Mrs Graham'
The Idlewild Trust
From Michael and Danice Iles,
    in memory of our parents
The Inch Family
E.M. Inglis
Marjorie Inglis, happy birthday
    mum with love
Mrs Sylvia Irvine
Lilla Jack
Margaret Jacks
Professor Ian Jackson and Dr Sally Cross
Mr and Mrs Lionel Jackson
Candida Jaco
Mike James

From James to Margaret, my
    eternal guiding light
Mr and Mrs J.P.A. Jameson
David and Patricia Jamison for
    their three granddaughters,
    Annabel, Emilia and Elysia
Gemma Jamieson
Dr Jane Jay
Celebrating Jean's life: family memories
R.F. Jeffrey
Dr Janet Jenkins, Edinburgh
Andrew MacAoidh Jergens
Claire Johns
Amaryllis Johnston
Dr Jack Johnston
Mary Johnston – for mum (a star)
Ms Maureen Johnston
In memory of Tom Johnston
Miss Jean Jolly
In loving memory of Derek
    Jones, love always, Helly
Ms Felicity Ann Jones
Maurice L. Jordan
Mrs Joyce Joy
In memory of Marie and Maurice Keane
To celebrate the 50th birthday of
    Yvonne Keith from her mother
Miss J.A. Kellett
Dr Norma Kellett
Mrs Elizabeth Kelly
Ella Kennedy
Mrs D.M. Kent
Miss Margaret Kerr
Susanna Kerr
Anne Kershaw
Michael G. Kidd
Mr Adam J. King and Ms
    Catherine K. McGlew
J.P. King
Anthony Kirkland
Mrs Jean Kirkpatrick
Dr Joanna Kitchin
The Lagneau Family
Jean, Peter and Louise Laing
The Lamb Family
Barrie and Janey Lambie
Joan S. Laverie
In memory of Graham C.
    Law from Isobel Law
Neville Lawther
Professor Donald Leach C B E from
    his wife Marilyn Jeffcoat

The Leckie Family
C.D. Leeming
The Lees Family
Joost Leeuwenberg
John Leighton
Robert Leith
Mr Gordon Leslie
Otto Leyde R S A, 1835–1897
Alison Linklater-Betley
The John Liston Charitable Trust
In memory of Mrs Anne
    Juliet Little 1933–2010
In memory of a much loved wife, mum
    and friend to many throughout
    the world, with love from Jack,
    Geneveive and John Livingstone
Robin Livingstone
Rosemary Lochhead
Mrs Jessie Lockhart
Dr Wolfgang Loeser
Jean and Geoffrey Lord
Sue and Graham Lorimer of Balerno, to
    celebrate the lives of Joy and Jim Petrie
Ian Lowson
To celebrate the life of Pamela Kathleen
    Lumsden, 24 July 1922 – 16 April 2009
In memory of Bill Lush and
    Jean Harvey Lush
Andrew and Evelyn Lyburn
May and Bill Lyle, in celebration
Lytham St Anne's U 3A Art
    Appreciation Group
Sheila MacAllister
To celebrate the 70th birthday of
    Norma Anne MacArthur
Peter Macaulay and Alan Rodger
Professor Viviene Cree for Calum
    and Iain MacDonald
Caroline MacDonald
David W.A. Macdonald
Patricia Macdonald
Lord Macfarlane of Bearsden
Ray Macfarlane
Gay MacGillivray
Mrs A. Macgregor
Dr Alexander MacGregor
Mr Stewart MacGregor
Mr and Mrs D. Gordon Macintyre
Angus and Elizabeth Mackay
Jessie P.W. Mackay
Miss Sheila M. Mackay
Mr Arthur Mackenzie
Miss Diana Mackenzie

In memory of Kenneth MacKenzie,
  Scottish Courts Service

Sheila and Ronald Mackenzie

Anne-Marie and Bill to celebrate
  our silver wedding

Mr Charles Mackintosh

Mrs J. Macleod

Mr Malcolm MacLeod

Catherine Macmillan

J. P. and Sarah Macpherson

Miss Julie-Ann Macqueen OBE

Mary Main

Barbara Malcolm

Norma Malcolm

The Malim Family

Mrs B.M.C Maniez

Anabel Marsh

Morag Marshall

Peter Marshall

Mrs Anne Martin

Colin Martin

Doreen Mae Martin

Mrs Margery Martin

Mrs Lesley Mason

Vincent, Christopher and Hilary
  Mason and family, Dumfries, to
  celebrate the life of Pat Mason

William Mathers

Isobel Johanna Matthee

George Maxwell Stuart – our
  grandson born 3 March 2011

To May from Ian

Dr Gordon McAndrew and
  Dr Leonora McAndrew

Andrew T McCabe

Ms Kerry McCall

For Molly Campbell McCathie,
  from her loving family

Dr Judith McClure and Dr Roger Collins

Mrs Brenda McConkey

The McCorquodale Charitable Trust

In memory of Charles Campbell
  McCorry, journalist, donated
  by his wife Cynthia Hay

Mr and Mrs Thomas McCracken

Mrs Evelyn McDonald

Brian McDonough

Mrs A. Rosemary McDougal

Catherine McDowall

Ishbel McFarlane

In celebration of the marriage of
  Mr and Mrs McGrattan

Harvey McGregor

Upon the harp do we give thanks for
  the life of Helen P. McGregor

Valerie McGuigan

Patricia McHale, Ilkeston, Derbyshire

Andrew McIntosh Patrick

Mrs Audrey McIntosh

Charles McIntosh

Finlay McIntosh

Jack McIntosh

Karina McIntosh

William Drummond McIntosh

Miss Bryony McIntyre

Professor Donald B. McIntyre, geologist

Mr and Mrs Ian McKee

Mr Christopher McKenna

Ian McKenzie Smith

Kenneth McKenzie

Muriel McKenzie

Mrs Kirsteen McKerrow

Ms Shelagh McKinlay

Mrs Mary McLaren

Fiona McLeod and Lorna Statham

Rod McLeod – a lovely man

The McMahon Family

David McNaughton

The McNeill Family, Glasgow, to
  celebrate the life of Myra Chestnut

Tilly McNeill

In memory of Alastair McNicol

Graham and Betty McNicol

Mrs Evelyn McPake

Dot McQueen

Professor R. McQuillin

Mr Jack McTigue

Jenifer Meek

A gift for Megan, Marion, Bethan,
  Ben, Toby and Olivia from Taid and
  Nain in their golden wedding year

Jill Meighan

Mr Alex Meikle

Amelia and Dewar Melvin

Dr and Mrs Malcolm Merrick

Professor David Michie

Mrs Cynthia Midgley

Mrs J. Millar

Kirsteen Millar

Mr Alan Miller

Margaret S. Miller

Shona Milligan

Mrs G. Mills and Dr Walter-Dressler

To celebrate the marriage of Jemma
  Mills and Steven D. Brown

Doreen Milne

Mrs Marie-Anne Milne

Ann Minto

This star is to remember my
  husband Brian J.L. Minto OBE,
  CA, from Margot J. Minto

In memory of Mary Minto,
  my stellar mum

Diane Mitchell

Mrs Dagne Moggie

Mrs Eunice G. Mole

Emily Montgomery

Mrs Margaret Moodie

Mrs Sheila Moonie

Miss Margaret Gordon Moore

Robert S. Moore

George Moore-Gwyn

Margaret R. More

Fiona and Nigel Morecroft

David and Sandra Morris

Alasdair Morton

To celebrate the birth of Penelope
  Lily Morton 27 September 2011

Alistair Mowat

John and Maxine Moy

Mr R.H. Paterson

To celebrate the life of Freida
  Muir 1918–2007

Simon and Dawn Muirhead

Helen and Morna Mulgray,
  the Mulgray twins

Margaret and Douglas Munro

Jennifer M. Munro

R. Munro

Sophie Munro: for the joy she has given

Teresa Munro

Tricia, Anthony, Caitlin and
  Lauren Murphy

Dr A.L. Murray

Mr and Mrs James Murray

Lorna Murray

Murrayfield View Residents Association

Rosemary and John Mutch

David and Vivienne Muxworthy

Alexander Nairne

John and Margery Naylor

Ms Isabel H. Neilson

Andrew Nelson

Rebecca Nelson

Andy and Ella Neustein

Elizabeth Nicholson

John Nicholson

Ms Junko Nishikawa

Dr Henry Noltie

Mrs Olive Norrie

Dr Brendan O'Connor

Fredrik N. Oldham born 5 July 2010

Maisie Lockhart Orr

Rosie Orr

Osprey Holidays

Helen Outram

To celebrate the lives of Andy and Evelyn Ovens, from Christine and Dot

Jerry Ozaniec

Professor and Mrs D. Parker

Dr Barbara Paterson

Miss Ruth Paterson

Sally Patrick

Remembering Isabel D. Patterson

Ron Patterson

To celebrate the 70th birthday of Christina Paulson-Ellis

Mr Colin Peacock

Pat and Roger Pears (Jessamy and Pauline and Andrew)

Mr Michael Pearson

Jim and Victoria Peers

Mrs Daphne Peirse-Duncombe

Mrs Elisabeth Penman

Mrs M.J. Petrie

Dr Sheena E. Petrie

Helena and Donald Pettie

PF Charitable Trust

Nicholas Phillipson

Mr John S. Pickles

Rose Pipes

Darryl Neil Michael Pithie

Neil Pithie

To celebrate John Porteous's 50th

Mary Porteous

The Portrack Charitable Trust

Grace Poulter

To celebrate the life of Nancy Powell from her family

Peter Powell – to celebrate forty years of the Thrie Estaits Antiques and Decorations

Jeremy Mitchell and Janet Powney

Alison May Preston MBE (What a star!)

Mr and Mrs Andrew Pringle

Martin Pringle and Marjorie Connell, to celebrate the life of Mrs Margaret Pringle

Anne Pritchard (née Cowe), who continues the family love of paintings

Lady Prosser

Mr and Mrs Andrew Purves

Ann Pyrkosz

Rhoda Quarmby

Mr and Mrs Dermott Quinn

Sarah Elizabeth Raikes

Miss Christine Ramage

Will Ramsay and Family

To celebrate the life of Michael Anthony Rand 1942–2009, an artist and printmaker, who came to Scotland to pursue his own work in the Highlands

Mrs Margaret Randall

Mrs Gerda Rankin

Mairi Rankin

Dr Jenny Rees and Mr Richard Rees

Philip Reeves

Alexander and Michaela Reid

Cadien Reid

Christine Lessels to celebrate the life of Helen Reid

Margaret Renton

Ms Annie Rhodes

To celebrate the sillyness and life of Edward Richards

Mrs Isobel Richardson

Alasdair Riley

The Ringham Family

Miss Diana Ritchie

June Ritchie

In memory of Lena Robb SRA, from Roy and Margaret Aitken of Spalding, Lincolnshire, and Andy and Liz Gill of Norwich

The Nancy Roberts Charitable Trust

Mr and Mrs Donald Robertson

Mrs E.F.S. Robertson, Ladybank, to celebrate the birth of Findlay G. Kung

Maeve Robertson

Miss Mary K. Robertson

Godfrey Robson

Dr Nigel Rose

The Earl and Countess of Rosebery

David Ross

Lord Ross

Hilary Ross

In memory of Steven Runciman

Mrs Irene Russell and Mrs Marlene Douglas

Patricia Rutherford

Helen Ruthven and Mike Angove

Dorothy Ryle

Tony and Eliza Sabine

Miss Ruth Sadler

David and Marilyn Salmon

The Saltire Foundation

Heather Salzen

Sarah A. Sandow

The Schaw Miller Family

Professor Bill Scott

Carol Scott

To celebrate the life of Derek J.R. Scott

In memory of Esme Scott

Mrs Margaret Scott

Stephen M. Seaman, to celebrate the life of Marjory Seaman

James Seaton

The Seligman and Stanic Families

Mrs Seton-Browne

Malcolm and Ann Shaw

Mr Murray Shaw

The Shearer Family

Gordon and Margaret Shiach

Mrs Daniella Shippey

Aurore and Jim Sibbet

Mr Frank Siersch

Anne and John Simmons

Richard Simon

Mr Jeffery Simpson

John Knox Simpson and Isabella Glasgow Lamond Simpson (née McLuckie)

Patrick and Henrietta Simpson

Helen Sims, in loving memory of my late husband, George Lister Sims

Roderick Sinclair

Rosie Sinden-Evans

Julia Singer, in memory of countless visits to museums and galleries together

Dr Wilfred Sircus and Mrs A. Caplan

To celebrate the birthday of Miss Sirui.W from Echi in 2011

Paul Skehel

Lydia and David Skinner to commemorate the work of Basil Skinner in the Scottish National Portrait Gallery from 1954–1966

Alastair and Carola Small

Dorothy Small

Bill Smith

Dennis and Jenny Smith

Edith S. Smith

Gillian Smith

Michael G.H.Smith

Patricia Smith

Mr David Smythe

Mrs Gill Smythe

For our Macmillan 'Star' Fiona Sneddon

The Society for the Protection
of Ancient Buildings

Soroptimist International of Edinburgh

Caroline Spurgin

Joan and Derek Stanton of Edinburgh

Judith Statt

In memory of the collection of
Stead and Margaret Stead-Ellis

Dr and Mrs David Steel

Mrs Alison Stewart

Colin Stewart

In honour of Professor Gordon
Stewart on his 90th birthday,
from his grandchildren

Mr I. and Mrs A. Stewart, Edinburgh

Iris Stewart

Jane Stewart and family

Professor John Stewart

Mrs Judith Stewart

Sir Moray and Lady Stewart

Lord Stewartby

Sir Jack and Lady Stewart-Clark

Angela Stockton and Suzanne Sullivan

Maureen Strachan

Dr and Mrs Duncan Strang

Miss Elizabeth Strong

Mrs Agnes H. Stuart

Frances Stuart

Mrs Rosemary Stubbs

Anne Sutherland

Evelyn, Duchess of Sutherland

Alvine Swanson

Dr Peter Symms and Mrs
Dorcas Jane Symms

Anna Colette Taylor

Carol Taylor

Katherine Maria Taylor

Mrs Margaret Taylor

Nicholas Teather

Tekoa Trust

Dr Christian Thin

Mrs Mary Thom

Kirsty and Euan Thomas, Edinburgh

Dougie and Beth Thoms

E. Thomson

Ian and Mary Thomson

Miss Margaret Thomson

Diana Thornton

Catrin Tilley and Rick Maizels – stars
for Ellie, Jack and Rory Maizels

Philip Tilling

Tramps like us…

Joyce Troup (To celebrate my Birthday!)

Emily Tupman

Robert and Elizabeth Turcan

Mrs Margaret Turner

Kitty Vaughn

Dame Lorraine Veitch Rutherford

Mr Michael D. Vickers

Mr Erik Vynckier

Allison Walker

David and Sheila Walker

Elise Leslie Walker

Fiona Walker

Mr and Mrs Ian Wall

Alexander Sturgeon Wallace

Ian Wallace

Ruth Walsh

Thomas Walsh

Alison Wardlaw

Ray, Anne and Linda Waring, in
memory of Mary Waring

Katherine Mary Warrender,
B63, Haddington, 2010

John and Mary Wastle

Miss Leonora Waterston

Kirsty Watherston

To celebrate the life of
William Eric Watson

Mollie and Julie Waugh

Miss Mary Webster

Lord Weir

Mrs Freda Whalley

Professor Roger Wheater OBE

Aileen Wheeler

Emma Whitaker

Charlotte and Harold White's
grandchildren

Dr Derek A. White

Mr John White

Pat White

T. George Wickham

Miss Joan Wilcox

To Ida Wilkie, to celebrate her 99th
birthday from the family

Kenneth C.B. Wilkie

Sheriff and Mrs A.B. Wilkinson

Gwenneth M. Williamson

Hil Williamson

Thelma and Charles Williamson

Peter and Jenny Willis

The HDH Wills 1965 Charitable Trust

Mrs A.G. Wilson

Alan Wilson

Alison Wilson, in memory of
my mother Moira Kimm

Mr Colin Wilson

Miss Elaine Wilson

Janet Wilson

Rhoda Wilson

Miss Vivien Wilson

To celebrate the life of Willie J.T. Wilson

Christine Windmill

Mrs Margaret Winter

Professor C.W.J. and Mrs A.M. Withers

The Alma and Leslie Wolfson
Charitable Trust

Women in Black, Edinburgh,
Stand for Peace

The Wood Family

Miss J.H. Wood

Dr Paul Muir Wood

Neil and Philippa Woodcock

Anthony Woodd

The Woods Family, Glenalmond College

Kerri Woods and Cristina Johnston

To celebrate the birth of Uist
Lennon Woomble

Mrs Lorna Wright

Elinor Wylie

Alexa Yan Hip

Margaret and John Yellowlees

To celebrate the life of Jarka Yeoman

To celebrate the birth of Ailsa Christina
Eleanor Young on 9 September 2011

Fiona Young

Georgie Young

Louise A.L. Young

Lynn Young

Anslie and Mary Yule

In memory of Millie Yule (née
Cartwright), mother of Jane and Sarah

*and all our donors who wish
to remain anonymous*

EXHIBITIONS

This is a listing of selected exhibitions and displays held at the Scottish National Portrait Gallery, Edinburgh from 1951 to 2009. An asterisk* indicates that the exhibition was accompanied by a publication.

1951

Scottish Literary Personalities of the 18th Century *

1952

Costume in Scotland in the 18th Century (with the Scottish Arts Council)*

1953

The Coronation of Charles II at Scone*

1955

Scottish Portrait Drawings 1750–1850 (with the Scottish Arts Council)*

Sarah Siddons – A Bi-centenary Display

Burns and his Contemporaries*

1956

Scottish Groups and Conversation Pieces (with the Scottish Arts Council)*

1958

Scottish Economists*

1959

Renaissance Decorative Arts in Scotland 1480–1650 (with the National Museums of Scotland and the Scottish Arts Council)*

1960

Acquisitions of the 1950s

1961

The Visit of George IV to Edinburgh in 1822*

Augustin Edouart Silhouettes – Centenary Exhibition

1962

Sport in Scotland*

1963

The Scottish Domestic Scene*

1965

The Jacobite Rising of 1715*

1966

Scots in Italy in the 18th Century*

1967

Mr Boswell (with the National Portrait Gallery, London)*

1971

A Virtuous & Noble Education*

1972

Acquisitions 1951–1971

1973

A View of the Portrait: Portraits by Alexander Moffat 1968–73*

1975

Painting in Scotland 1570–1650*

1976

Childhood in Seventeenth Century Scotland*

A Face for any Occasion*

1977

The Making of a Royal Portrait: HM The Queen in Thistle Robes

1978

John Henning (with Paisley Museums)*

Van Dyck in Check Trousers*

1979

Women in Scotland 1660–1780*

1980

Eye to Eye*

Scottish Empire*

Method and Madness – Richard Dadd's Portrait of Alexander Morison*

Jessie Ann Matthew – Photographer

1981

Seven Poets: Hugh MacDiarmid, Norman MacCaig, Iain Crichton Smith, George Mackay Brown, Robert Garioch, Sorley MacLean and Edwin Morgan – Paintings and Drawings by Alexander Moffat and Photographs by Jessie Ann Matthew (from the Third Eye Centre, Glasgow)*

1982

John Michael Wright, The King's Painter*

The Gentle Eye – Photographs by Jane Bown (from the National Portrait Gallery, London)*

Some Statesmen of the Great War*

1983

Bill Brandt (from the National Portrait Gallery, London)*

Action Portraits*

1984

Karsh of Ottawa: 50 years of Photographs by Yousuf Karsh (from the National Portrait Gallery, London)*

Scotland's Story (with s t v)*

1985

Treasures of Fyvie*

France in the National Galleries of Scotland. Henri-Pierre Danloux (1753–1809): A French Painter in Exile*

Scottish Photography – The First Half

1986

Masterpieces of Photography from the Riddell Collection*

James Tassie 1735–1799: Portraits of the Enlightenment*

Printed Light: The Scientific Art of William Henry Fox Talbot and David Octavius Hill with Robert Adamson (with the Science Museum, London)*

Sir Alexander Gibson: Portraits by John Houston

1987

Genial Company (with Nottingham University)*

A Celebration of Mary, Queen of Scots: The Queen's Image*

A Celebration of Mary, Queen of Scots: The Queen's World*

William Carrick: 19th Century Photographs of Russia

Sir Adam Thomson: Portraits by John Wonnacott*

1988

Contemporary Scottish Photography

The Photography of John Muir Wood*

Photography in Scotland 1938–88

Masterpieces from the Edinburgh Photographic Society

Photographs by James Cox 1849–1901*

1989

Thomas Annan's Old Closes and Streets of Edinburgh*

William Adam 1689–1748 (from the Royal Incorporation of Architects in Scotland)*

Patrons and Painters: Art in Scotland 1650–1760*

The Man who Shot Garbo: The Hollywood Photographs of Clarence Sinclair Bull (from the National Portrait Gallery, London)*

A Vision of India: Frederick Bremner

1990

Portraits in Fashion: Photographs by John Swannell

William Donaldson Clark: Edinburgh in the 1850s*

How to Take a Portrait

Julia Margaret Cameron

Dynasty: The Royal House of Stewart (with the National Museums of Scotland)*

John Zephaniah Bell*

Portraits from the Riddell Collection

New Scottish Photography*

1991

Francis Frith's Egypt

Scottish Photographers Abroad

The Art of Jewellery in Scotland (with the National Museums of Scotland)*

The Great Newhaven Project:: Hill & Adamson's 'Fishermen and Women of the Firth of Forth' (also shown at the Musée D'Orsay, Paris)*

Los Todos Santeros: Photographs by Hans Namuth

1992

Kenneth Macleay: Landscapes, Portraits and Miniatures*

Portrait of the Artist

Allan Ramsay 1713–1784 (also shown at the National Portrait Gallery, London)*

The Art of the Photographer, J. Craig Annan (shown at the Scottish National Gallery of Modern Art)*

Stones of Venice: Ruskin's Venice in Photographs*

Scotland Observed: A Decade of Collecting

1993

Eugene Impey: A Passage through India*

Phoebe Anna Traquair*

Photographing Children*

The Art of the Daguerreotype

1994

'One little room…an everywhere': A Photographer's Choice: David Williams*

Annie Liebovitz Photographs 1970–1990*

Visions of the Ottoman Empire*

Class of '49: Photographs by Lida Moser

Sir James Gunn 1893–1964 (also shown at The Fine Art Society, London and Harris Museum and Art Gallery, Preston)*

1995

Paul Strand, The World on my Doorstep*

Light from the Dark Room (shown at the Royal Scottish Academy)*

Richard & Maria Cosway: Regency Artists of Taste and Fashion (also shown at the National Portrait Gallery, London)*

The Carrick Family in Russia

1996

Authentic Portraits of Robert Burns

John Kobal Photographic Portrait Award

Speaking Likeness: Voices from Scotland's Past and Present*

David Livingstone and the Victorian Encounter with Africa (shown at the

Royal Scottish Academy; from the National Portrait Gallery, London)*

George Rodger: Photographs from Africa (shown at the Royal Scottish Academy)*

David Roberts RA: A Bi-centenary Display*

Look, Love and Follow: Prints and Medals of the Jacobite Cause (also shown at Duff House)*

Portrait Miniatures from the Collection of the Duke of Buccleuch*

Double Vision: 19th Century Stereoscopic Photography

1997

Signs and Wonders: Photographs by Owen Logan

John Kobal Photographic Portrait Award

The Face of Denmark*

Raeburn. The Art of Sir Henry Raeburn 1756–1823 (shown at the Royal Scottish Academy; also shown at the National Portrait Gallery, London)*

Eve Arnold: In Retrospect*

Women in White. Photographs by Lady Hawarden*

Portraits of Excellence: Photographs of Academics from the University of Edinburgh*

1998

Whippet Racing and Other Photographs

The Science of the Face*

David Williams: Findings…Bitter/Sweet

John Kobal Photographic Portrait Award

Edward Piper: Circles of Stone

The Winter Queen, The Life of Elizabeth of Bohemia 1596–1662*

Little Sparta: Portrait of a Garden (photographs by Robin Gillanders)*

William Klein's New York*

Prophets and Pilgrims, Ruskin, Proust and Northern Gothic

1999

Raeburn's Rival: Archibald Skirving 1749–1819*

Kenny Hunter

Curve: Mark Johnston*

O Caledonia! Sir Walter Scott and the Creation of Scotland*

Political Contemporaries

Murray Johnston's Landscape*

Caroline Rye, The Turin Machine

Magna Brava: The Magnum Women Photographers*

2000

Health of the Nation

A Shepherd's Life (paintings by Victoria Crowe)*

Young Entrepreneurs

The Art of the Documentary

Men of the Clyde: Stanley Spencer's Vision at Port Glasgow*

Wish I Was Here

Writers of our Time

Significant Others

2001

Narcissus: Twentieth Century Self-Portraits

Thomas Carlyle: a Hero of his Time

Josef Breitenbach

Portrait Miniatures from the Clarke Collection*

The King Over the Water: The Life of Prince James Francis Edward Stuart 1688–1766*

Return to life: A New Look at the Portrait Bust (with the National Portrait Gallery, London and the Henry Moore Institute, Leeds)*

The Fine Art of Photography

Larry Towell: The Mennonites*

A Tribute to Edwin Morgan

2002

Great Houses of Scotland*

An Exile's Eye: The Photography of Wolfgang Suschitzky*

Portrait Miniatures from the Dumas Egerton Collection*

Medical Portraits

Facing the Light: The Photography of Hill and Adamson*

Stephen Lawson, Photographing Time

Scots in Film: Portraits by Donald Maclellan

The Golfers*

Calum Colvin – Ossian, Fragments of Ancient Poetry*

On Top of the World: Scottish Mountaineers at Home and Abroad

2003

Navigating Stevenson: Digital Artworks by Sara Gadd*

Portrait Miniatures from the Daphne Foskett Collection*

Mad, Bad and Dangerous: The Cult of Lord Byron*

Maud Sulter, Jeanne Duval: a Melodrama*

The Dream Team

High Society. The Life and Art of Sir Francis Grant 1803–1878*

Parallel Lives: Where Past Meets Present

Terrain: Landscapes of the Great War by Peter Cattrell

Fay Godwin: Landmarks*

2004

Patrick Geddes: The French Connection*

Below Stairs: 400 Years of Servants' Portraits (with the National Portrait Gallery, London)*

Portrait Miniatures from the National Galleries of Scotland*

Once Upon Our Time. Portrait Miniatures by Moyna Flannigan*

My Family (from Family Mediation Scotland)

Modern Women

Keeping Faith

Scotland's Women

2005

A Tale of Two Cities

Twelve Poets at Edinburgh Park*

Our Highland Home: Victoria and Albert in Scotland*

The Healing Touch: 500 Years of Scots in Sickness and Health

The Philosopher's Garden (photographs by Robin Gillanders)*

Portrait Miniatures from the Merchiston Collection*

Cut and Dried: Harry More Gordon and Augustin Edouart

Portraits from The Scotsman's Collection – Editors and Proprietors of the Scotsman Newspaper

William Wallace: Scottish Patriot 1305–2005

B P Portrait Award (from the National Portrait Gallery, London)*

Ghosts by Cai Guo-Quiang

2006

Thoroughly Modern Women

Fizzers: The Alternative Portrait Gallery*

Stranger than Life: 400 Years of Caricature

Portrait Miniatures from Scottish Private Collections*

The Face of Craft: Portraying Scotland's Makers*

Out of Dialogue: George Wylie

Being There: Harry Benson's Fifty Years of Photojournalism*

Energy: North Sea Oil Portraits (paintings by Fionna Carlisle)*

2007

Shotgun Wedding: Scots and the Union of 1707*

Entrepreneurial Scotland*

Force: a Contemporary Portrait of Scotland's Police (photographs by Jane Brettle)*

The Naked Portrait (also shown at Compton Verney, Warwickshire)*

Paintings in Crayons: Pastel Portraits from the National Galleries of Scotland

Photography in India in the Nineteenth Century

Demarco's Festival*

Telford: Father of Modern Engineering

Dieter Appelt: Forth Bridge – Cinema. Metric Space*

B P Portrait Award (from the National Portrait Gallery, London)*

2008

The Somnambulists*

Faces and Places: Creating and Recording Scotland's Buildings

Heroes: Nineteenth Century Self-help Role Models (with the National Library of Scotland)

Vanity Fair Portraits (from the National Portrait Gallery, London)*

John Muir Wood: The Origins of Landscape Photography in Scotland

The Intimate Portrait (with the British Museum, London)*

Parallel Lives 2

Homecoming

The Face of Scotland: The Scottish National Portrait Gallery at Kirkcudbright (shown at Kirkcudbright Town Hall)*

2009

The Face of Scotland: Masterpieces from the Scottish National Portrait Gallery (shown at The Fleming Collection, London)*

Rough Cut Nation*

2010

Portrait of the Nation (shown at the Scottish National Gallery)

KEEPERS OF THE GALLERY

JOHN MILLER GRAY (1850–1894)
Curator 1884–94

SIR JAMES LEWIS CAW (1864–1950)
Keeper 1895–1908
(also Director, National Galleries of Scotland 1907–30)

THOMAS CORSAN MORTON (1859–1928)
Keeper 1908–25

STANLEY CURSITER (1887–1976)
Keeper 1925–30
(also Director, National Galleries of Scotland 1930–48)

ARCHIBALD HASWELL MILLER (1887–1979)
Keeper 1930–52

ROBERT EDWARD (ROBIN) HUTCHISON (b.1922)
Keeper 1953–82

DR DUNCAN THOMSON (b.1934)
Keeper 1982–97

JAMES HOLLOWAY (b.1948)
Keeper 1997–2012
(the post of Keeper was renamed Director in 2000)

INDEX OF PERSONS

This index contains the major contributors to the history of the Portrait Gallery as well as other significant figures mentioned in the text. Subjects and artists of works in the collection are not included, nor are individuals still living.